EUROPEAN MILITARY CRISIS MANAGEMENT

Connecting ambition and reality

BASTIAN GIEGERICH

ADELPHI PAPER 397

The International Institute for Strategic Studies

Arundel House | 13–15 Arundel Street | Temple Place | London | WC2R 3DX | UK

ADELPHI PAPER 397

First published October 2008 by **Routledge**
4 Park Square, Milton Park, Abingdon, Oxon, OX14 4RN

for **The International Institute for Strategic Studies**
Arundel House, 13–15 Arundel Street, Temple Place, London, WC2R 3DX, UK
www.iiss.org

Simultaneously published in the USA and Canada by **Routledge**
270 Madison Ave., New York, NY 10016

Routledge is an imprint of Taylor & Francis, an Informa Business

© 2008 The International Institute for Strategic Studies

DIRECTOR-GENERAL AND CHIEF EXECUTIVE John Chipman
EDITOR Tim Huxley
MANAGER FOR EDITORIAL SERVICES Ayse Abdullah
ASSISTANT EDITOR Katharine Fletcher
PRODUCTION John Buck
COVER IMAGE PA

Printed and bound in Great Britain by Bell & Bain Ltd, Thornliebank, Glasgow

British Library Cataloguing in Publication Data
A catalogue record for this book is available from the British Library

Library of Congress Cataloging in Publication Data
A catalogue record for this book is available from the Library of Congress

ISBN 978-0-415-49419-9
ISSN 0567-932X

Contents

GLOSSARY

CHG 2008	Civilian Headline Goal 2008 (EU)
CHG 2010	Civilian Headline Goal 2010 (EU)
DRC	Democratic Republic of the Congo
ESDP	European Security and Defence Policy
EUMS	EU Military Staff
FOC	full operating capability
HG 2003	Headline Goal 2003 (EU)
HG 2010	Headline Goal 2010 (EU)
ISAF	International Security Assistance Force (Afghanistan)
MEADS	Medium Extended Air Defence System
TEU	Treaty on European Union
WMD	weapons of mass destruction

INTRODUCTION

Crisis-management missions, which are usually undertaken by a multi-national force, involve a variety of activities, including military ones, aimed at creating or maintaining a secure environment in order to enable peace to be established and/or to end a crisis. They include traditional peacekeeping missions, peace-enforcement and peace-making missions, stabilisation and reconstruction missions, conflict-prevention missions and humanitarian operations. Missions are mandated or authorised by the UN Security Council and carried out under the auspices of various international organisations, such as the UN itself, NATO, the European Union (EU) or the African Union or, sometimes, by coalitions of states or (very rarely) by states acting alone. There has been a dramatic growth in such missions over the past 20 years: almost 80% of the operations authorised by the UN since 1948 were launched between 1988 and 2007.

Worldwide demand for missions continues to grow rapidly, and demand for troops continues to outstrip supply. In 2007, around 160,000 troops were deployed for crisis management through the UN and other organisations, including NATO and the EU. It is estimated that UN operations alone would need some 200,000 personnel each year in order to sustain current levels of deployment.[1]

It is difficult to precisely measure the gap between demand and supply because different types of shortfall exist, some of which are harder to quantify than others. Some shortfalls are clear, such as in missions in Afghanistan and Sudan, where the number of deployed troops lags behind the number specified in commanders' assessments. Other deployments have turned out to be much smaller once under way than initial military estimates deemed that they needed to be. A more intangible, though no less real, shortfall can be seen in those missions for which planning never even begins, despite a need for them, because it is anticipated that it will not be possible to generate the required force.

Since the pressure of increasing demand for crisis-management missions is unlikely to lessen in the near future, it is clear that troop-contributing governments and the international organisations that serve as frameworks for multinational missions – the 'international community', for want of a better phrase – need to increase their force-projection and intervention capacities. Like other Western democracies, EU member states, because of their wealth, relative military competence and commitment to human rights, bear a particular responsibility for expanding the international community's capacity for action. In 2007, some 63,000 EU member-state troops were deployed in international crisis-management roles, just over 4% of total active forces in the Union. This is hardly an impressive percentage given the EU's ambition, outlined in the 2003 European Security Strategy, to play a major role in global security and in promoting peace and stability.[2]

Many states, particularly those in Europe, are in the process of reorienting their armed forces from a primary focus on the defence of national territory or the territory of allies to greater emphasis on the projection of armed force overseas, including beyond alliance territory, for crisis-management purposes (albeit with varying degrees of success). This reorientation ought to mean that, overall, the international capacity for military crisis management will steadily increase. However, it seems that each year the international community is more stretched by the demand for crisis missions. Of course, international military engagement will always be selective. EU member states and others are not expected to intervene in every crisis, nor should they be. 'Selectivity is an inherent, and prudent'[3] aspect of international crisis management. Nevertheless, a strong argument can be made that 'were military capacity not such a severe constraint, the international community might well have been willing to intervene in a number of additional conflicts',[4] based on the merits of each case.

Against this background, then, what is the EU's level of ambition for crisis-management operations? Brigadier-General Reinhard Trischak asked this question in 2007 in his capacity as director of the Concepts and Capabilities Division of the EU Military Staff (EUMS), and suggested that it continued to defy a clear answer.[5] Certainly it would appear that the

EU is devoting considerable energy to crisis management. The European Security and Defence Policy (ESDP), under which the Union conducts civilian and military crisis-management operations, was launched in 1999 and entered its operational phase in 2003. Since 2003, the EU has launched more than 20 missions in and beyond Europe. Military and civilian headline goals have been defined and revised. Strategic planning assumptions and illustrative scenarios have been drawn up for the types of mission the EU would want to conduct. Catalogues of military requirements have been compiled in extraordinary detail and EU members have pledged capabilities towards them. Pledges have been scrutinised in relation to needs, and the resulting shortfalls have been identified. Also in 2003, the EU adopted its European Security Strategy to provide guidance on the overall role the Union wishes to play in the security realm.[6]

Thus, the military-technical groundwork for the ESDP has been completed, and a basic political-strategic notion of its purpose exists. The policy has given the EU the institutional and political framework to become a prominent international crisis-management actor. As a result, what the EU wants to be able to do militarily in international crises, how often, for how long, with how many troops, under what conditions and where – in other words, an outline of its level of ambition – can be fairly precisely calculated and contrasted with its actual achievement.

Such comparison reveals that there is a disconnect between what the ESDP is supposed to be able to do and what it in fact does. The former chief executive of the EU's European Defence Agency, Nick Witney, recently remarked that 'EU leaders commit to ambitious defence goals and deadlines, celebrate inadequate outcomes, move the goalposts, and authorize a further round of "reviews" and "roadmaps"'.[7] Analysts have observed that 'to date ... EU-led operations have been rather tentative'.[8] EU crisis-management operations have indeed been limited, both in size and objective, compared to the Union's ambitions. And while they have in general been successful within the limits set for them, they have also been marred by planning and implementation problems, despite taking a risk-averse approach that tends to shield troops from the most challenging situations.[9] What accounts for this disconnect between ambition and reality?

Because the effort a country makes is discretionary, tension between national and international priorities regularly inhibits military crisis-management efforts, and is very likely to continue to do so for the foreseeable future. A prominent example is force generation, the process by which contributing nations designate the military assets and capabilities required for an operation and make them available to the operation commander. The EU points out that it is at the mercy of its member states as regards force generation. A June 2008 document outlining its force-generation system states that:

> Member States' ... political commitment, which later translates into appropriate military assets and/or capabilities offered, constitutes a key for the success of an operation. Without significant offers from [member states], the Force Generation process cannot be accomplished and an EU-led military operation cannot be launched.[10]

Experience shows that even for limited crisis-management operations of the kind that the EU has conducted in the past, force generation is messy and challenging. Many required assets and capabilities do in fact exist among member states' resources, but, as Nick Witney has put it, 'the commitments tend to evaporate when the pledges [made towards EU headline goals] are called in'.[11] For example, during the EU operation in the Democratic Republic of the Congo (DRC) in 2006, requirements for medical support and tactical airlift (both rotary and fixed-wing) were only met after several force-generation conferences and individual appeals to particular EU members: a German officer has recently remarked of this operation that 'the planning for EUFOR RD Congo was characterized from the outset by navigating the delicate balance between political objectives and constraints on the one hand and military requirements on the other'.[12]

Anyone who has visited Brussels and asked questions about force-generation problems in ESDP missions will be pointed in the direction of two explanations: lack of capabilities and lack of political will. The former is a well-understood problem, and one which will continue to create significant obstacles, in particular should the EU choose to conduct more demanding ESDP operations. The latter, by contrast, tends to be treated almost as an immutable force, something beyond the control of Brussels itself. It is the latter that is the root cause of the disconnect between ESDP ambition and reality.

Though the need for cooperative crisis management is becoming ever more pressing, as long as the relevant security challenges do not amount to existential threats to EU states, the level of effort that each state makes will remain discretionary. And any military coalition, whether formal or ad hoc, depends on the commitments made by its members for its capacity for action. The Union's ambitions will never be achieved if they are not supported by or at least compatible with member states' national conceptions of what armed forces are for. As NATO's Deputy Assistant Secretary General for Policy and Planning Major-General Heinrich Brauss, who has also held a senior position in the EUMS, clarifies: 'collective defence planning cannot guarantee the delivery of capabilities for specific ongoing operations nor is it the panacea for force generation ... It is all about political will and public support'.[13]

States' ambition and performance: the 'crisis-management profile'

Surprisingly little is understood about how nations come to determine their commitments and the kinds of constraints on contributions that are at work. It is important to try to advance understanding of the differing levels of national ambition that exist in this area, and of how countries variously perform in military crisis-management operations. Greater such understanding ought to enable an evaluation of the prospects for an upwards convergence of policy across the EU that could enhance the Union's crisis-management capacity.

This paper explores the domestic and international determinants of European states' commitments and performance, and their implications for multinational crisis-management capacity under the ESDP. On the domestic side, political, legal, societal, bureaucratic and economic factors all play a role. On the international side lie the pressures of direct or indirect security threats, relationships with other countries, and cooperation frameworks such as the EU, NATO and the UN. (Regarding these cooperation frameworks, however, it is important to remember that while member governments are involved in drawing up the ambition levels of organisations such as NATO and the EU, such efforts at collective defence planning do not tend to definitively shape national efforts.)

Determining a state's 'level of ambition' for crisis management is a complex task. Factors that need to be considered include the state's current and past crisis-management-force pledges to international organisations. Levels of ambition can also be expressed in terms of the tasks that a country's White Papers, security strategies and defence doctrines expect its military to perform in crisis-management missions. There has been very little work done directly addressing the question of what influences levels of ambition for international crisis management. One notable exception is a research paper published in 2006 by the Austrian Ministry of Defence that argued that ambition levels are a consequence of the international position of a state in terms of geography, prestige and involvement in international organisations.[14] The study also emphasised the importance of a state's national security culture, and its capacity for action as determined by domestic public opinion and institutional decision-making processes, as well as the availability of adequate means.[15] The complex interplay of these variables produces the national level of ambition. With some adaptation, the study's conclusions offer a useful framework for understanding the goals states set themselves in this area. Ambition can be understood largely as the output of a political system dealing with a diverse set of internal and external pressures. Of course, levels of ambition are just one part of the story. Similar factors also affect states' operational records. Clearly, ambitions and performance ought to be intertwined, each one influencing the other. Together, they form what is termed here a 'crisis-management profile'.

Determinants of ambition and performance

To begin with the international determinants of state ambition and performance, it is generally agreed that the international security environment is becoming increasingly complex and threats ever more diffuse. It might therefore be thought that cooperation among countries would become correspondingly more difficult, as approaches to dealing with this environment diversified as well. However, while there is an element of this, the opposite dynamic also seems to be at work.

Because the characteristics of the security challenges that EU member states now face make any effective response to them extremely complex, the incentives for cooperation in international organisations have in fact increased. These characteristics include asymmetric tactics, the non-state, anonymous status of some of the actors involved and a geographic diffusion and interconnectedness of threats that has prompted one academic observer to speak of a 'threat continuum'.[16] It seems that diversified threats increase the tendency for inter-state cooperation because no country can ensure its security in isolation.

Crisis management is of course a prime manifestation of this kind of international cooperation. It is designed in part to protect EU member states from the instability generated by crises and conflicts across the world, by managing them when and where they occur rather than waiting for knock-on effects such as terrorism, the proliferation of weapons of mass destruction (WMD) and organised crime to reach Europe.[17] As well as this interest-based rationale, crisis management is also motivated by the desire to end or prevent human-rights violations.

The expectation of cooperation generated in international frameworks (primarily the EU and NATO in the European context) is an important external factor influencing national ambitions and achievements. In formulating goals, aspirations and the institutional and operational capabilities to deal with international challenges through the framework of the EU, the ESDP has given rise to an institutional structure of its own, representing a significant cluster of permanent bodies working within the security realm.[18] Although these bodies are almost exclusively staffed by personnel seconded from EU member states who remain accountable to national governments, the constant interaction of these individuals at an EU level can be expected, over time, to produce an overlap in their respective positions. An ESDP culture distinct from national outlooks thus emerges, which may ultimately feed back to national capitals. At the same time, while the ESDP is certainly an important reference point for national policymakers, and governments expect to have to justify the decisions they make in relation to the policy, the intergovernmental nature of arrangements means that EU-level goals in this area cannot be pushed through against the will of national governments.

The internal determinants of a country's crisis-management profile can be broken down into the following elements: institutional decision-making processes, military means available (i.e., existing capabilities and defence spending) and societal factors. To begin with institutional processes, differences among countries' institutional arrangements – including variations in the roles and relationships of policymakers – can lead to different methods of security- and defence-policy formation, initiation and implementation. An understanding of the effects of these institutional factors is aided by focusing on those aspects most relevant to the use of force, such as whether or not there is parliamentary involvement in decision-making. Some institutional arrangements make action in this sphere more likely than others.

Clearly, crisis-management profiles are influenced by available resources: it is sensible to expect policymakers to define ambitions in terms of the means they know are available. It is important, however, not to assume that known means always define the limits of a country's ambitions and performance, which are the result of the interplay of all the factors discussed here. For example, policymakers might set ambitions that necessitate the acquisition of new or improved means.

The strategic and broader political culture is another important domestic factor. State policymakers generally approach the use of force in largely predictable ways that are rooted in the national identity and historical experience of the society in question. For example, in some countries, such as the United Kingdom, the use of force is viewed as an acceptable foreign-policy tool, while in others, such as Germany, there is a deeply ingrained reluctance to use force for purposes other than territorial or collective defence. Naturally, a country's national security culture manifests itself beyond its strategic community in political discourse and public opinion. These in turn feed back into the policymaking culture.

Taken together, institutional factors, available means and national security cultures form a wide array of internal pressures, which can either add to or counter the external pressures outlined above. Thus, national policymakers must engage at both an international and a domestic level simultaneously, to try to establish links between the two levels and balance the opportunities, constraints and demands arising at each.[19] Since a state's external use of armed force must be legitimated in a domestic decision-making process, domestic factors can be expected to exert more influence than international ones in the formation of national crisis-management profiles. Thus, in states in which domestic parameters are favourable to international demands, ambitions will be precisely defined and performance levels high. Governments that are faced with a clash between international and domestic demands may seek to avoid precisely defining their ambition levels, and will register low or medium performance. They are also more likely to renege on international commitments.

The use of military force is changing its character and international crisis-management missions, whether undertaken through the ESDP, NATO, the UN or a coalition arrangement, are increasingly becoming the structuring purpose of EU member states' armed forces.[20] Because efforts towards these missions are discretionary, national crisis-management profiles are at the core of the problem of how to increase multinational crisis-management capacity. While the ambitions of the EU in this area have become clear over the past few years, the Union is falling well short of its declared goals. Almost ten years after the birth of the ESDP, in the face of growing demand for international crisis management, a better understanding of how national and international agendas support each other and of how progress is blocked by differences is desperately needed. Serious work in this area must be undertaken in order to expand European capacity for action and start to close the gap between ambition and reality.

CHAPTER ONE

EU Crisis Management: Ambitions and Achievements

The 2003 European Security Strategy does not define an explicit level of ambition for military crisis management. It simply states that the Union 'should be able to sustain several operations simultaneously'.[1] It expresses an aspiration that EU security policy should have global reach: 'The European Union has the potential to make a major contribution, both in dealing with ... threats and in helping realise ... opportunities. An active and capable European Union would make an impact on a global scale.'[2] Though the strategy has been much criticised for failing to clearly define means–ends relationships and hence failing, in some eyes, to be a strategy at all, the document does offer an outline guide to what the EU should be seeking to achieve and how. It states that the EU needs 'to develop a strategic culture that fosters early, rapid, and when necessary, robust intervention'[3] in crisis situations, including with military means. The implication of this is that the EU should have the military capability, through its member states, to be able to confidently handle conflict situations and the tasks covered by the ESDP.

The ESDP was created in 1999 in order to strengthen the EU's Common Foreign and Security Policy. The task spectrum it is intended to cover is defined by the so-called Petersberg tasks, which were first drawn up in 1992 within the framework of the Western European Union and later incorporated into the Treaty on European Union (TEU) by revisions made at the EU summit in Amsterdam in 1997. These cover humanitarian and rescue operations, peacekeeping and crisis-management tasks, including peace-making, to be undertaken by combat forces. The European Security Strategy expanded this task spectrum, and the Treaty of Lisbon, which had been intended to enter into force in 2009 following ratification by all member states, offered a further revised definition of what the ESDP was to cover. The Lisbon Treaty stipulated that the EU should use both civilian and military means to conduct humanitarian, rescue and joint-disarmament operations, provide military advice and assistance to third countries and undertake conflict prevention and peacekeeping. It also specified that the Union should be able to apply combat forces to crisis-management tasks including peacemaking and post-conflict stabilisation. The treaty observed that all these tasks could be applied to the fight against terrorism, and that the EU could use ESDP missions to support third countries combating terrorist activity in their territories. Whether or not the Lisbon Treaty enters into force, this expanded definition of the task spectrum has now been accepted as guiding the ESDP.

Headline goals past and present

Further clues to current and recent EU crisis-management ambitions are given by the various 'headline goals' that have been adopted as planning targets by EU member states since 1999. At the June 1999 European Council meeting, EU governments agreed that 'the Union must have the capacity for autonomous action, backed up by credible military forces, the means to decide to use them, and a readiness to do so, in order to respond to international crisis without prejudice to actions by NATO'.[4] This was refined into Headline Goal 2003 (or HG 2003, also known as the Helsinki Headline Goal) at the December 1999 Council meeting: 'cooperating voluntarily in EU-led operations, Member States must be able, by 2003, to deploy within 60 days and sustain for at least 1 year military forces of up to 50,000–60,000 persons capable of the full range of Petersberg tasks'. In an annex to the presidency conclusions of the Helsinki meeting,[5] member governments elaborated that the force should be 'militarily self-sustaining with the necessary command, control and intelligence capabilities, logistics, other combat support services and additionally, as appropriate, air and naval elements'.[6] It is clear from this that HG 2003 involved a larger pool of personnel than the core 50,000–60,000 envisaged for the crisis-management force.

At the time that HG 2003 was defined, the EU had not yet developed its own illustrative scenarios (contingencies posited by militaries for planning purposes), and its strategic-planning assumptions, including about the concurrency of operations, were underdeveloped. A document from early 2000 assumes that 'the most demanding [missions will] occur in and around Europe. Forces should also be available and able to respond to crisis worldwide, albeit at lesser scale'. The document also suggests that the Union 'should plan to be able to conduct a single corps-sized crisis management task, while retaining a limited capability to conduct a small-scale operation ... Alternatively [the EU] should prepare to maintain one longer term operation at less than the maximum level and at the same time be able to conduct another operation of a limited duration'.[7] At this stage, the EU was still focused on large-scale operations in and around Europe. No doubt the Kosovo crisis of 1999 had a shaping impact on these assumptions.

At the December 2000 European Council meeting in Nice, there was already substantial political pressure to declare the ESDP operational. As early as 2001, the Council declared the EU capable of conducting some crisis-management missions, even though the criteria for HG 2003 were far from being met. In May of the deadline year, the Council, unable to declare HG 2003 met, nevertheless implied that the EU could conduct missions across the whole Petersberg-task spectrum, while conceding that the ESDP was limited by significant capabilities shortfalls.[8]

Having missed the 2003 headline-goal deadline, the EU Council defined a new target, Headline Goal 2010 (HG 2010), in May 2004. It is very different to HG 2003 in that it does not focus at all on numbers. Member states presented this as a new focus on quality rather than quantity. The main commitment of HG 2010 was 'to be able by 2010 to respond with rapid and decisive action applying a fully coherent approach to the whole spectrum of crisis management operations covered by [the TEU]'.[9] While the overall aspiration thus became more obscure, one central element of the new headline goal was a concrete innovation: the creation of so-called EU 'battlegroups'. These are rapid-reaction-force packages of between 1,500 and 3,000 personnel (including all enabling capabilities), deployable for up to 120 days if resupplied, and equipped and trained to cover tasks at the more demanding end of the Petersberg-task spectrum. With HG 2003 neither met nor abandoned as HG 2010 was launched, the EU's assumptions about how the ESDP would be implemented appeared in 2004 to be in flux. The fact that the representative of the French EU presidency issued a reminder more than four years on, in the second half of 2008, that the HG 2003 agenda still existed, illustrates that this uncertainty still to some degree remains.[10]

Initially, the ESDP was driven by the logic of military crisis management, and development of civilian components was slow. Their eventual

formulation resulted in the comprehensive approach to crisis management advanced in the European Security Strategy, which acknowledges
that multifaceted contemporary security threats require a correspondingly
diversified response involving many instruments. The strategy states that
the EU 'is particularly well equipped to respond to such multi-faceted situations'.[11] Its potential to create a truly integrated crisis-management tool,
combining civilian and military means, has since been the great promise
of the ESDP. It is this potential that gives the EU its comparative appeal as
a global crisis-management actor.

The EU Council drew up Civilian Headline Goal 2008 (CHG 2008)
in December 2004 to tackle the civilian aspects of crisis management. As
with the military headline goals, member states were invited to pledge
personnel towards the CHG 2008, but national contributions were not
compulsory. The goal envisaged that some civilian capabilities would be
deployable within 30 days of a decision to launch a mission. Capabilities
could be deployed autonomously, jointly (that is, integrated with) or in
cooperation with military capabilities. The CHG 2008 states that 'the EU
must have the ability to conduct concurrent civilian missions at different
levels of engagement ... including at least one large civilian substitution
mission at short notice in a non-benign environment', and acknowledges
that 'civilian crisis management missions may need to be sustained over
a longer period of time' than originally planned for.[12] Subsequent documents make clear that the Council operates on the assumption that up to
five civilian missions would need to be conducted simultaneously.

Although the CHG 2008 itself does not have an explicit numerical
target, the EU's civilian level of ambition can be calculated by adding up
the personnel numbers specified in more detailed planning documents
to work out what would be required to conduct five missions across the
civilian-capability priority areas identified in the headline goal – that is,
across policing, rule of law, civilian administration, civil protection and
monitoring. A total of some 18,200 civilian personnel with 477 different
job descriptions would be needed to conduct five missions along the lines
specified in the CHG's illustrative scenarios: 13,265 police; 2,558 rule-of-
law officials; 1,421 civilian-administration personnel; 764 civil-protection
experts and 198 monitors of the security and political situation. By comparison, the UN had some 9,500 police deployed across its missions in 2007, a
figure that was set to rise by around 4,000 in 2008.[13]

The final report on the CHG 2008 concluded that the requirements of
recent and ongoing ESDP missions had not been entirely reflected in the
headline goal's assumptions. With real-world ESDP operations becom-

ing more diverse and their functional and geographical scope expanding since they began in 2003, a review was deemed necessary. Thus, a Civilian Headline Goal 2010 (CHG 2010) was launched in late 2007, its timeline pegged to that of the military HG 2010.[14] The CHG 2010 follows directly on from CHG 2008, and does not involve a complete revision of targets like that seen in the military realm. Instead, the new civilian headline goal seeks to improve the quality and availability of capabilities, while developing the work done towards its predecessor. A review of illustrative scenarios and assumptions and an audit of capabilities is to be undertaken as part of the work towards CHG 2010.

Scenarios, planning assumptions and capabilities development

Headline goals do not in themselves indicate precise levels of ambition because they do not give details of the specific missions envisaged. The EUMS conducts the detailed military planning, under the supervision of the EU Military Committee.[15] At the beginning of the EU capabilities-development process is a set of illustrative scenarios. Each scenario involves a different set of assumptions about the following strategic-planning variables: the distance of the theatre of operations from Brussels; the time required to reach full operating capability (FOC); the duration of the mission; and, for long-term operations, force-rotation arrangements. Currently, the EU uses five illustrative scenarios for military crisis-management planning, discussed below.[16]

Separation of Parties by Force
This scenario involves combat forces undertaking crisis-management tasks, including peacemaking. Thus, it entails activities at the upper end of the Petersberg-task spectrum. The planning assumptions for the scenario are that the theatre of operations would be up to 10,000km from Brussels (operations with a distance of 4,000km and 6,000km are also planned for) and that it would take at least 60 days to establish FOC. This reaction time implies that theatre-entry elements would be deployed within a shorter time frame. The deployment is assumed to last up to six months, hence there would be no requirement for rotation of forces, although it is also assumed that the mission to separate parties by force would be followed by a smaller stabilisation and reconstruction mission.

Stabilisation, Reconstruction and Military Assistance to Third Countries
This scenario covers peacekeeping, election monitoring, institution building, security-sector reform and support to third countries combating

terrorism. The planning assumption is that the mission would be conducted up to 10,000km from Brussels (a 4,000km version of the scenario has also been planned). FOC is to be reached within 90 days, and the assumption is that the mission would be sustained for at least two years, thus requiring several personnel rotations.

Conflict Prevention
Conflict prevention covers preventive engagement, preventive deployment and embargo, counter-proliferation and joint disarmament operations. It is assumed that operations would take place up to 10,000km from Brussels (there are also plans for operations at 4,000km), and that FOC would be reached within 60 days of a decision to launch. Conflict-prevention operations are assumed to last for at least one year, requiring the rotation of forces.

Evacuation Operation in a Non-Permissive Environment
This covers the evacuation of non-combatants. As EU member states will always want to be in a position to be able to conduct such operations no matter where the crisis occurs in the event that EU citizens are at risk, versions of the scenario for up to 10,000km and up to 15,000km from Brussels have been planned. Rapid reaction is extremely important in evacuation operations, so the planning assumption is that an initial operating capability would be reached no later than ten days after the decision to launch a mission. The duration of the mission would depend on circumstances, but is expected to be short – no longer than 120 days – so troop rotation would not be needed. The scenario assumes that the mission would need to evacuate between 2,000 and 10,000 non-combatants.

Assistance to Humanitarian Operations
This scenario covers both management of the consequences of disasters and atrocity prevention. As in the evacuation scenario, the planning assumptions are that missions would be conducted at a distance of up to either 10,000km or 15,000km from Brussels, and that initial operating capability would need to be reached no later than ten days after the decision to launch. Humanitarian operations are not expected to generate a requirement for rotation, and the scenario assumes a duration of up to six months. Operations are expected to need to deal with between 75,000 and 100,000 evacuees and refugees.

These scenarios and the strategic-planning assumptions of which they are composed are the basis on which EUMS planners compile lists of the military assets and capabilities required to conduct missions. The process of compiling such lists has been gone through once since the ESDP's inception: in the event that new scenarios are added, it will be undertaken afresh. Requirements are expressed in terms of generic force packages and 'reference units' (which denote military units or assets delivering a specific capability). Many packages and units were planned in great detail, in several cases right down to platoon and section level.[17] From these lists, the EUMS drew up the 'Requirements Catalogue', which lists the precise units and assets needed to conduct the operations identified in the scenarios within the parameters of the strategic-planning assumptions. Member states were then invited to pledge contributions to the requirements outlined in the catalogue. Pledges were scrutinised and compiled in a 'Force Catalogue', which describes in qualitative and quantitative terms what member states have pledged towards the headline goal. Pledges from non-EU countries, of which there are some, are not included in the Force Catalogue.

A comparison of the two catalogues shows the shortfall. Shortfalls can be due to the absence of the necessary assets and capabilities from member states' inventories or, since pledging for such missions is a voluntary process, to member states' unwillingness to pledge resources they do possess. The implications of the shortfall for operations covered by the scenarios are detailed in a document rather misleadingly known as the Progress Catalogue (none of these catalogues is in the public domain). From the drawing up of the illustrative scenarios to the compilation of the Progress Catalogue, this process represents a complete cycle of EU military-capabilities planning.

As its logistics-support concept for military operations makes clear, the EU expects its troops to operate in demanding environments with little or no host-nation support, a harsh climate and challenging terrain.[18] As far as troop requirements are concerned, Separation of Parties by Force would be a large-scale operation, with the Stabilisation, Reconstruction and Military Assistance and Conflict Prevention scenarios falling into the medium category, and evacuation and humanitarian assistance requiring small-scale deployments. Interviews with officials in Brussels and documents seen by the author indicate that the EU has drawn up three 'concurrency suites', or plans detailing the types of operation its forces should be able to conduct near-simultaneously. While the force requirements of the concurrency suites remain classified, it may be assumed that each suite requires an initial deployed land force significantly larger than the 50,000–60,000 personnel envisaged in HG 2003, given that the Separation of Parties by Force scenario alone would require a force of that size. If the rotation of personnel that would be necessary for medium-scale operations (Stabilisation, Reconstruction and Military Assistance and Conflict Prevention) is also taken into account, the total personnel pool needed is considerably larger than is commonly understood. Thus, despite the failure to meet HG 2003, it is clear that EU member states have upgraded their overall level of ambition for military crisis management. HG 2010 involves more tasks, more troops, quicker reaction times over longer distances and more demanding concurrency suites.

A similar planning process takes place on the civilian side, although it is less integrated with the military side than might be wished. Five civilian illustrative scenarios were developed in 2005, later than and independently of the military ones. These are: Stabilisation and Reconstruction (there are two stabilisation and reconstruction scenarios, one with a substitution mission and one without[19]); Conflict Prevention, with particular emphasis on monitoring and on supporting the offices of EU Special Representatives; Targeted Strengthening of Institutions; and Civilian Support to Humanitarian Operations. As in the military field, these scenarios have been used to formulate mission tasks and compile lists of required personnel. Pledges have then been made by EU member states and compared to the identified requirements. Though the methodology used in the civilian field is similar to that used in the military, important elements of the capability-planning process, such as deciding on the number of missions to operate concurrently, formulating strategic-planning assumptions and, indeed, defining desired end states have been undertaken separately for the civilian realm.[20] Now that both civilian and military branches have run through complete cycles of their respective processes, however, there are likely to be attempts to coordinate the two more closely. One step currently under consideration is that of drawing up a single set of illustrative scenarios for both civilian and military planning purposes.

Overall, military operations short of collective defence have been defined and planned for in great detail at the EU level. Furthermore, despite the relatively short lifespan of the ESDP, these ambition levels have already been revised upwards. This is particularly striking given that the operational record of the ESDP is very limited, and the EU has as yet come nowhere near attaining the upper regions of its ambition.

Operational record

The core institutional framework for launching and running military crisis-management missions through the ESDP was established in 2000 when the European Council created three permanent bodies based in Brussels.

Table 1: **ESDP operations since 2003**

Mission	Location	Duration	No. of personnel	Type
Africa				
Operation Artemis	DRC	2003	1,800	Military
EUSEC RD Congo	DRC	Since 2005	40	Civilian–military
EUPOL Kinshasa	DRC	2005–2007	30	Civilian
Mission to support AMIS II (African Union mission)	Sudan	2005–2006	50	Civilian–military
EUFOR RD Congo	DRC	2006	2,400	Military
EUPOL RD Congo	DRC	Since 2007	39	Civilian
EUFOR Chad/CAR	Chad and Central African Republic	2008–2009	3,700	Military
EU SSR Guinea–Bissau	Guinea–Bissau	2008–	39	Civilian–military
Asia				
AMM	Aceh/Indonesia	2005–2006	225	Civilian
EUPOL Afghanistan	Afghanistan	Since 2007	230	Civilian
Europe				
EUPM	Bosnia-Herzegovina	Since 2003	182	Civilian
Concordia	Former Yugoslav Republic of Macedonia	2003	400	Military
EUPOL PROXIMA	Former Yugoslav Republic of Macedonia	2004–2005	200	Civilian
EUFOR/*Operation Althea*	Bosnia-Herzegovina	Since 2004	2,500 (initially 7,000)	Military
EUPAT	Former Yugoslav Republic of Macedonia	2006	30	Civilian
EUBAM	Ukraine/Moldova	Since 2006	69	Civilian
EULEX Kosovo	Kosovo (planned)	2008–	1,900	Civilian
Caucasus				
EUJUST THEMIS	Georgia	2004–2005	10	Civilian
EUMM Georgia	Georgia	2008 (October) to 2009	300	Civilian
Middle East				
EU BAM Rafah	Palestine	Since 2005	27	Civilian
EUJUST LEX	Iraq/Brussels	Since 2005	25	Civilian
EUPOL COPPS	Palestine	Since 2006	31	Civilian

Sources: Council of the European Union, 'Aperçu des missions et opérations de l'Union Européenne', June 2008; IISS, *Military Balance* and *Strategic Survey*, various editions.

These were the Political and Security Committee, the Military Committee and the EUMS.[21] The Council retains ultimate control over the activities of these bodies. Below them, an operation commander implements the missions that are decided on. The three permanent bodies, the Council and the operation commander are together responsible for crisis-response planning, and between them they handle the political-strategic, military-strategic and operational, as well as the tactical, aspects of planning.

The ESDP has been operational since 2003, with EU personnel conducting 22 crisis-management missions to date, 14 of which have been purely civilian (see Table 1). It seems clear that the Union is in the process of trying to achieve two major goals through the ESDP: to establish an autonomous (i.e., independent of NATO) capacity for action in the field of crisis management, and to enhance its profile as a credible global security actor.

To a substantial extent, it has succeeded in drawing nearer to these goals. The EU has established itself as an international crisis-management body, and a distinct demand for EU crisis-management missions has developed. The appeal of the EU resides in the high level of political legitimacy it represents, its perceived neutrality and its economic strength. The Union is now also an established civil–military actor, and the wide spectrum of its available means is unique in the field, meaning that it has the potential to dominate integrated crisis management in the future.

Nevertheless, many capability shortfalls remain. What do the operations undertaken thus far tell us about the major trends and aspirations in EU crisis management?

Global ambition

Moving away from its original focus on Europe, the EU has steadily increased the operational reach of its forces since operations began in 2003. The Balkans and Africa, where the greatest numbers of EU personnel are deployed, are clear focal points. The Middle East is another key region for ESDP operations, and EU personnel have also been deployed to Asia. At roughly 10,000km from Brussels, the 2005–06 AMM mission to monitor the peace agreement in Aceh is the farthest-flung EU venture there has been thus far.

Expanding scope of missions

Alongside the extension of its geographical scope there has been an expansion of the EU's task spectrum, which has become increasingly diverse. This has particularly been the case in the civilian sector. Policing missions, missions to uphold the rule of law, border-control missions, security-sector-reform missions and active disarmament missions have all been conducted in recent years. These have ranged in size from ten personnel up to the 1,900 planned for EULEX Kosovo.

Military operations so far rather limited

All operations have been modest in terms of numbers, with the largest, *Operation Althea*, which had an initial strength of 7,000, being conducted with recourse to NATO assets and capabilities and following on from a NATO mission. Doubts therefore remain about the EU's capacity for autonomous action beyond relatively small operations. The EU has also been rather risk averse in the military arena so far, though it is not fair to assert, as some commentators have, that the Union usually relies on other organisations to pacify combatants.[22] While it is the case that NATO was militarily engaged in the Balkans before the ESDP had even been launched, it is also true that European troops deployed to Africa to support the UN with bridging operations in actually or potentially deteriorating security situations while the UN built up its capacity. Nonetheless, the five military ESDP missions that have been completed or are currently under way have involved a total of only 15,200 troops, including the initial 7,000-strong *Althea* in Bosnia. In mid 2008, some 6,200 troops were deployed under the EU flag, which amounts to less than 0.4% of the active forces of EU member states. Furthermore, no military operation has been conducted further than (just over) 6,000km from Brussels (Kinshasa, DRC).

Blurring of civil–military boundaries

It is one of the goals of the ESDP to undertake more crisis-management operations that blur the classic distinction between the civilian and military spheres. The 2005–06 peace-agreement-monitoring mission in Aceh, though it involved mostly military personnel operating in a civilian capacity rather than a truly 'integrated' force, is one example of such an operation, as is the explicitly hybrid mission in support of the African Union in Sudan and Somalia in the same period. The EU hopes that there will be more mixed operations, and internal pressure to coordinate planning to this end is expected to increase. There appear to be plans to develop mission-specific financial arrangements to replace the current separate procedures that exist for each field. But the EU has not thus far lived up to its own expectations for integrated civil–military crisis management. Very few missions have involved a mix of personnel, and those few were very limited in scope and size (all were between 40 and 50 strong). These missions were a far cry from the kinds of operation to which the EU aspires: fully integrated operations in which significant civilian support is offered to military operations.[23] The need for integrated or 'one-stop shop' missions is well recognised by both the European Security Strategy and national policy documents, as contemporary crises require the application of a wide spectrum of instruments. However, the operational record of the ESDP shows that the EU is not yet able to provide such a capacity.

Multinationality

ESDP missions tend to be made up of small contingents of personnel from several different contributor countries. The EU's latest military mission, EUFOR Chad/CAR, is typical. By July 2008, a total of almost 3,250 troops had been deployed by 24 countries. The three largest contributors accounted for some 2,400 troops (France 1,671, Ireland 408, Poland 299), with the remaining 850 coming from no fewer than 21 contributing nations.[24] EUFOR RD Congo in 2006, which peaked at around 2,400 personnel, drew contingents from 23 contributing nations. High levels of multinationality increase legitimacy and provide a seat at the table and the opportunity to influence events to many countries. However, there is tension between a high degree of multinationality and operational effectiveness. The more contributing countries there are, the greater the chances that at least some will come with national restrictions on the tasks they are allowed to carry out. In addition, multinational cooperation always causes some friction, even if units from different countries are accustomed to training and exercising together. Some contingents, particularly the smaller ones, may not have their own command-and-control capacities, which can complicate the job of force commanders.

'End date rather than end state'

It is in the nature of most complex crisis situations that it is not clear before the medium or long term whether or not a mission is working, and many situations require ongoing attention. However, in the civilian field, there is no opportunity for long-term secondments of personnel such as, for example, police officers or judges, mainly because their deployment abroad leaves an – expensive – hole to be filled at home. In the military field, there is a pronounced tendency to tightly define the duration of a mission, to the point of naming a fixed exit date that may not, when the time comes, be appropriate in view of the military situation on the ground. Contributing governments in most EU member states seek clear exit dates mainly because of the cost of more protracted deployments and their concern about the fragility of any domestic consensus in support of deployment. Alongside the sense of the importance of being seen to do something in response to crises is an unwillingness to commit significant resources over an extended period of time. One officer involved in planning for EU operations has remarked sharply that 'sometimes it feels as if we are conducting missions to satisfy our consciences rather than achieve a certain effect on the ground'.[25]

The danger that leaving on time might be accorded more importance than getting the job done well is not something over which operation commanders have any control, as they must operate within the strategic frameworks they are given by EU member governments, acting through the Council and the Political and Security Committee.

Case study: EU bridging operations in the DRC

In 2003 and 2006, EU forces intervened in conflict situations in the DRC for limited periods of time at the request of the UN. The first mission, *Operation Artemis*, was conducted with France providing command and control, and the second, EUFOR RD Congo, was led by Germany. Both operations were carried out without recourse to NATO assets but benefited greatly from access to airports in several African states, which were used as staging areas, and access to French bases near the area of operations.

It is worth examining these two missions in some detail for what they can tell us about the EU's aspirations and accomplishments in this field, in part because they are to date the only military missions that the EU has undertaken and completed autonomously. They were also conducted outside the EU's immediate neighbourhood, and thus may offer a better sense of likely future ESDP missions than the two military missions the EU has led in the Balkans (where it followed NATO engagement). Finally, both missions illustrate the problems the EU faces in relation to force generation, capabilities and political will among EU member states, while at the same time showing that the EU does not only engage militarily in completely pacified situations.

Operation Artemis

Operation Artemis was a symbolically important mission, because it demonstrated for the first time the EU's ability to conduct an autonomous operation beyond the European continent and in a demanding environment. The operation was launched on 12 June 2003, following UN Security Council Resolution 1484, passed on 30 May 2003. France had been the first to respond to the UN request to intervene, offering to send personnel on the condition that the mission would have a robust mandate (Chapter 7 of the UN Charter), be welcomed by countries in the region and be limited in time and scope. With agreement on these points secured, France then decided on reflection to multinationalise the operation by making it an ESDP mission.[26] The mission was attractive to participants because it had clearly set limits on the key parameters of size, duration and responsibilities.

The mission's mandate was to protect refugee camps housing internally displaced persons, to secure the airport in Bunia (the capital of the northeastern province of Ituri, where hostilities were most frequent and severe) and to guarantee the safety of the civilian population and international personnel in the city of Bunia. The mission, along with the UN force that was already in the DRC and awaiting reinforcement, had been recommended in a special report of the UN Secretary-General that had stressed the need for comprehensive UN engagement in order to move the peace process forward despite continuing violence in the DRC.[27] It was designed as a stopgap measure to fill in while the reinforcement of the UN mission was being prepared. Its area of operations was limited to Ituri province. In accordance with its mandate, the force ceded its responsibilities on 1 September 2003 and handed over to the reinforced UN force. *Artemis* at its peak consisted of 2,200 troops, the majority of which were provided by France. Contingents also came from Belgium, Germany, Sweden and the UK, and the non-EU states of Brazil, Canada and South Africa.

Logistics and support

Airlift for *Artemis* was provided by Airbus 310 and DC-8 aircraft and chartered Antonovs 124 using Entebbe airport in Uganda.[28] From Entebbe, tactical airlift to Bunia was undertaken using C-130 and C-160 aircraft. Forty-four Antonov flights from Europe to Entebbe, each with an 85-tonne load, and 220 flights from Entebbe to Bunia were needed to deploy personnel and equipment. The key contributors to the airlift operation were France and Belgium and, from outside the EU, Brazil and Canada. Ground forces consisted of some 1,000 regular troops, mostly French, as well as 150 French and 80 Swedish Special Forces. The regular troops were equipped with armoured personnel carriers, 120mm mortars and lightly armoured vehicles, and were supported by an engineering company. Further support was provided by a Belgian surgical unit, a German A-310 air ambulance on standby and four helicopters (two French and two South African). Twelve French *Mirage* aircraft equipped for ground-attack missions and ready to provide close air support were based in Chad and Gabon, along with a number of French tanker aircraft, and a French *Atlantique* surveillance aircraft was stationed at Entebbe. French and British engineers were tasked with the preparation and maintenance of Bunia airfield. They built around 10,000m² of aircraft parking and repeatedly resurfaced the runway in order to enable the tactical-airlift operation.

Operations and incidents

An important element of *Artemis* operations were the 'presence' and 'show-of-force' operations undertaken by the ground forces, who took control of crucial intersections and patrolled throughout Bunia, regularly augmented by *Mirage* overflights. Although it was not widely reported, *Artemis* ground forces also repeatedly engaged in fire fights with militia factions. On 13 June 2003, a convoy of 70 troops and 15 vehicles found itself between fighting militias, and reported incoming small-arms fire, mortars and rocket-propelled grenades. After the EU force returned fire and *Mirages* conducted overflight missions in a show of force, the militias disengaged. Three days later, a Special Forces detachment came across a small group of plundering militiamen, two of whom were killed in the ensuing confrontation. On 11 July, while around 200 *Artemis* troops were searching a militia base for weapons to be confiscated, a platoon among them was engaged by some 200 militiamen. The Europeans responded, reportedly killing several militiamen and neutralising the base. European forces, especially Special Forces detachments, repeatedly exchanged fire with militia groups during the remainder of the operation's mandate, killing a further 20 and sustaining no losses.

Resources and shortfalls

Artemis was dependent on the combat support provided by its own engineers. Local infrastructure was inadequate even for the comparatively light force the Europeans deployed. Had the mission required a heavier deployment of armoured units, combat support would have become a severe challenge, complicating transport arrangements and necessitating even greater improvements to local infrastructure. Though it was able to access the necessary assets through charter arrangements, the operation also highlighted Europe's shortage of strategic-lift capacity.

Achievements

Bearing in mind its limited remit, *Artemis* was successfully implemented. The mission by and large maintained control of its area of operations, and no major incidents or deterioration of the security situation occurred while the force was in place. When challenged, *Artemis* forces proved willing to engage in combat, and showed clear superiority over local opponents, though such confrontations were localised and of short duration. Security in Bunia improved over the course of the deployment, several militia groups were successfully contained and there is evidence that *Artemis* successfully disrupted the supply lines of some such groups. Furthermore, a sizeable number of refugees were able to return home, and significant quantities of humanitarian aid were delivered. However, its limited area of operation, relatively small size and short duration meant that the mission's impact was largely a short-term one. The geographical restrictions on *Artemis* meant that the violence it apparently quelled was merely temporarily displaced to areas outside Bunia. When the UN force took over in September 2003 with lesser capabilities, the security situation deteriorated. Thus, while *Artemis* had performed well according to its mandate, the broader strategy for securing peace and stability it had been intended to support was only marginally advanced.

EUFOR RD Congo

In April 2006, the EU Council approved a military mission to help ensure security around presidential elections in the DRC, which were scheduled for 30 July 2006. Once again, the EU was deploying a temporary force in support of a UN mission in the DRC (MONUC on this occasion), this time with Germany as the lead nation. EUFOR RD Congo reached its peak strength in mid August with 2,466 deployed troops.[29] Twenty-one EU member states participated, along with non-EU states Turkey and Switzerland. The four largest contingents came from France (1,090), Germany (730), Poland (130) and Spain (130).

Logistics and support

A reserve based in Libreville, Gabon, consisted of one French and one German–Dutch infantry task force. The air component was also stationed at Libreville. This consisted of fixed-wing tactical airlift provided by Belgium, France, Germany, Greece, Italy, Portugal and Turkey (four C-130s and two C-160s, plus three C-130s stationed in Europe but available upon request), and a French fighter detachment of two *Mirage* F1s and one KC-135 tanker. A German–French–Swiss medical unit, a French–German combat service support company and a French signals detachment completed the Libreville base. A French–Swedish–Portuguese Combined Joint Special Operations Task Force was stationed in Port Gentile, Gabon, and a French battlegroup served as the dedicated strategic reserve in Europe.

Command and control came from an operational headquarters in Potsdam in Germany (staffed initially by German personnel and later by personnel from other force-contributing nations, seconded there for the duration of the mission), and a force headquarters in the DRC supported by a French company. A Spanish company with anti-riot capabilities served as an immediate reaction force in Kinshasa and a similarly equipped Polish force-protection company focused on VIP protection. There was also a French signal company and a German signal detachment. Germany provided intelligence, surveillance, target-acquisition and reconnaissance capabilities, as well as tactical lift (three CH-53 helicopters), and a Belgian company provided unmanned aerial vehicles. In addition there was a German–French–Austrian psychological-operations detachment, a German–French–Polish civil–military cooperation team and a multinational medical unit. The deployment of EUFOR required 133 strategic movements lifting 11,000 tonnes.

Operations and achievements

Central to EUFOR's activities were the information operations conducted by the psychological-operations detachment. These included the deployment of an advance information team to counter negative rumours about EUFOR objectives and capabilities. Contact was made with international humanitarian organisations, local non-governmental organisations and government agencies in order to provide information on EUFOR and convey the message that it could provide a safe environment both for politicians and the population at large.

In August 2006, EUFOR deployed a combined infantry and special-operations contingent of 186 troops and 26 vehicles to Kananga, a town some 850km east of Kinshasa. This was a show-of-force operation intended to demonstrate to potential election spoilers and militia groups that the force could deploy to remote locations in a timely manner. When fighting between supporters of the two presidential candidates broke out in the same month, EUFOR reinforced MONUC's efforts to establish order and separate the fighting camps, helped to recover diplomats trapped by the fighting and mediated between the warring factions. In another operation, it airlifted weapons out of an area in which weapons caches had been found alongside groups of demobilised soldiers. In order to prevent violent outbreaks as the election results were reported, EUFOR deployed almost all of its on-call theatre reserve to Kinshasa as the results began to appear. Also during the mission, EUFOR conducted air reconnaissance missions using *Mirage* F1 fighters, which were ready to provide close air support if needed.

The DRC missions underlined for the EU the importance of tactical airlift, rapid-manoeuvre capabilities, information operations and engineering and combat support, all of which, in giving forces the flexibility they needed, proved vital for the successful conduct of the missions. Yet the force-generation process for *Artemis* and EUFOR revealed how difficult it was to obtain commitments for crucial assets and capabilities from member states. For example, it took two weeks to close a gap in EUFOR's medical team: two surgeons were needed.

Artemis and EUFOR also raised questions about the adequacy of EU operational planning and command-and-control arrangements for EU-led operations: since the EU does not have a permanent planning and control capacity of its own, operational planning can only begin once an operational headquarters has been designated, which can cause delays and introduce further elements of uncertainty into the force-generation process. *Artemis* benefited greatly from French leadership and the fact that France, initially considering a unilateral intervention, had already conducted much of the planning for the deployment before the EU had agreed to launch an ESDP mission. However, this is clearly not the kind of scenario that can be relied upon to replicate itself in future.

Overall, militarily, these were limited operations that produced limited results within the parameters of what they set out to do. From a political point of view, their main achievement was symbolic: they demonstrated the EU capacity for action in general and, specifically, in support of the UN. While this kind of achievement builds confidence and adds to the body of shared ESDP experience among EU member states, the long-term impact of the missions on peace and stability in the DRC is less clear.[30]

Ambition versus performance

The ESDP has already undergone significant development in the field of operations. In terms of the increasing diversity and geographical reach of missions, this development has been largely positive. However, some of the tendencies outlined above show that member states need to address a range of challenges if they want to live up to their collective aspirations. The EU's potential for robust engagement and the strategic gain that its missions represent for European security and for the regions in which missions have been conducted remain unclear.

The Union is building up credibility and experience – and thus political weight – in the security realm through its ESDP operations. Yet there is a contradiction between the image of an increasingly self-confident actor and the quantitative and qualitative limitations of ESDP missions to date,

Table 2: **EU military level of ambition versus military operational record**

	EU level of ambition	Operational record	Level of ambition met?
Type of mission	Separation of Parties by Force, Stabilisation, Reconstruction and Military Assistance, Conflict Prevention, Evacuation, Humanitarian Assistance	Stabilisation, Reconstruction and Military Assistance, Conflict Prevention	No
Distance from Brussels	Up to 15,000km	Up to 6,000km	No
Reaction time	As little as ten days, no more than 90 days	Rapid reaction not yet truly tested	No
Duration	120 days to two years +	120 days to two years +	Yes, although at low force levels
Force requirement	60,000 +	6,200 (August 2008)	No

a contradiction that is due in part to restrictions on resources. The limited interest shown by European governments in international crisis management ought to ward off any complacency about the EU's potential in this area. Furthermore, ESDP missions have not yet been confronted with significant opposition in an area of operations, and there is a risk that their comparative success thus far could lure mission commanders and personnel into a false sense of security, leaving them unprepared for any major confrontation.

It is also not clear that procedures and decision-making would hold up under the time pressures of a true crisis situation. It is not yet apparent how much strain ESDP operations can take. Its operational achievements to date have presented the EU with a dilemma: success so far has bred high expectations, which the EU can only satisfy by accepting greater risks than it has in the past. Equally, though, a major setback in the field is likely to have wide political repercussions. The question is, therefore, whether the EU will in future seek out crises appropriate to the instruments it has available, or whether it will actively seek greater resources to be able to tackle more challenging situations.

Notwithstanding the clear progress of the past five years, it seems probable that the reality of the EU as a global security actor will continue to diverge from its aspirations. In spite of its high abstract level of ambition, operationally, the EU has preferred to tread very carefully, and there is little sign that this will change in the near term. It is difficult to disagree with Nick Witney's assessment that 'the issue with the operational record as a whole is its lack of ambition'.[31] So far, ESDP operations have been so limited in their objectives and size that their relative success should not come as a surprise. Their achievements, while clearly marginally useful, have been nowhere near commensurate with the Union's stated ambition to be a major global-security actor. Furthermore, the fact that even the modest missions conducted so far have encountered embarrassing commitment problems during force generation, with implications for mission objectives and duration, underscores the serious practical limitations that exist on EU action in this area.

CHAPTER TWO

National Ambitions and Performance

Over the past ten years, there has been a trend towards increasing the force-projection capabilities of Europe's national armed forces. For most countries, this amounts to a paradigm shift in military thinking, as forces gradually move their focus away from territorial defence towards overseas deployment for crisis-management purposes. However, within this trend, there is a tension between the immediate operational demands imposed by an increased tempo of deployments and the long-term process of reconfiguring forces for expeditionary purposes. The urgent, sometimes unforeseen requirements of current expeditionary operations and the cost of ongoing operations put additional strain on the resources available to fund the overall transformation of forces.

Across the EU, member states are at different stages in the process of change, and display varying priorities. An all-out embrace of expeditionary missions as the key purpose of armed forces and a correspondingly high ambition level for overseas deployments is rare. Most countries try to build greater projection capability while retaining territorial defence as one of the military's central missions, if not *the* central mission.

Nevertheless, force structures have changed significantly over the past decade or so in line with the increased focus on expeditionary missions. There has been a clear trend towards smaller militaries, with the percentage of national populations serving in the armed forces declining across Europe. In 1995, of the 27 countries that are now members of the EU, six had armed forces that accounted for more than 0.8% of the population.

Table 3: **Current EU member states: active armed forces as percentage of population and conscripts as percentage of active armed forces, 1995 and 2007**

Country	1995		2007	
	Percentage of population active armed forces	Percentage of active forces conscripted	Percentage of population active armed forces	Percentage of active forces conscripted
Austria	0.70	44.84	0.48	52.02
Belgium	0.47	0	0.38	0
Bulgaria	1.21	50.34	0.55	0
Cyprus	1.35	87.00	1.26	87.00
Czech Republic	0.83	46.76	0.22	0
Denmark	0.63	25.08	0.54	22.66
Estonia	0.23	75.71	0.31	33.41
Finland	0.61	76.85	0.55	65.53
France	0.70	46.26	0.41	0
Germany	0.42	40.39	0.29	23.04
Greece	1.64	66.55	1.46	32.26
Hungary	0.69	67.38	0.32	0
Ireland	0.36	0	0.25	0
Italy	0.57	53.15	0.31	0
Latvia	0.27	Unknown	0.25	0
Lithuania	0.24	Unknown	0.38	15.52
Luxembourg	0.20	0	0.18	0
Malta	0.50	0	0.40	0
Netherlands	0.48	37.23	0.27	0
Poland	0.72	56.75	0.33	31.48
Portugal	0.55	32.47	0.43	20.36
Romania	0.95	48.16	0.33	0
Slovakia	0.87	Unknown	0.31	0
Slovenia	0.42	65.48	0.29	0
Spain	0.53	61.17	0.36	0
Sweden	0.73	49.38	0.26	32.5
UK	0.41	0	0.29	0

Sources: IISS, *The Military Balance 1995/96* (Oxford: Oxford University Press for the IISS, 1995); IISS, *The Military Balance 2008* (Abingdon: Routledge for the IISS, 2008).

The forces of a further 11 fell into the 0.5 to 0.79% category, and ten had comparatively small forces comprising less than 0.5% of the population.[1] By 2007, this picture had changed completely: only two countries – Cyprus and Greece, both involved in the ongoing territorial dispute over Cyprus – continued to maintain armed forces comprising more than 0.8% of the population and only three (Bulgaria, Denmark and Finland) fell into the middle category. No fewer than 22 out of the 27 now maintained comparatively small active armed forces accounting for less than 0.5% of their populations.[2]

There was also a marked shift away from conscription over the same period. In the context of the Cold War, European armed forces used conscripts to guarantee the manpower deemed necessary to defend territory and deter aggression. In 1995, only five countries – Belgium, Ireland, Luxembourg, Malta and the UK – had all-volunteer forces.[3] By 2007, this number had risen to 16, meaning that a clear majority of EU member states now has all-professional militaries.[4] Small all-volunteer forces, better suited to a force-projection posture than large conscript-based forces because of their comparative mobility and the high levels of training undergone by professional soldiers, have become the dominant organising principle of Europe's armed forces.

National defence doctrines and reviews reflect the variety of approaches to the role of the military that can be found across the Union; it is a more variegated picture than a cursory glance at these trends might suggest. For a minority of countries, including Greece and Finland, territorial defence remains the overriding concern. A sizeable group, including the Czech Republic, Hungary and the Netherlands, also rank territorial defence first, but explicitly acknowledge participation in international crisis-management missions and domestic assistance to civilian authorities in the case of disasters or major accidents as other key tasks. These three broad categories of activity together make up the definition of the armed forces' role in the majority of EU member states.

A number of states, including Austria and Germany, have argued that crisis management and territorial defence are of equal importance. This argument has on occasion been used to justify undertaking restructuring and re-equipment programmes to increase force-projection capability at the same time as maintaining essentially redundant structures in the name of territorial defence. Major reorganisation will always face a degree of bureaucratic inertia and resistance from elements anxious to preserve the status quo. Another approach, most prominently expressed in the 2008 French White Paper on Defence and National Security,[5] holds that much the same capabilities are needed for all military activities; hence it is not necessary to rank those activities according to importance. Finally, the UK stands out in embracing force projection as the overarching purpose of its armed forces, a position it took as early as 1998 in that year's Strategic Defence Review.[6]

Thus, while broad indicators relating to force structures suggest that European armed forces are being moved in a similar direction by their governments, national aspirations for the use of armed forces and the operational record show enormous variety.

State levels of ambition

The national 'level of ambition' here refers to a state's expression of the maximum military contribution it intends to make to international crisis-management missions. This is of course distinct from the effort a country anticipates it would make in a territorial- or collective-defence scenario. Given that international crisis-management missions are not conducted to combat a direct existential threat to the contributing nation, governments will only ever make a part of a country's total capability available for them. The size of that contribution will depend on a mixture of factors, some of which relate to the demands and expectations of the international environment, while others – the dominant ones – are domestic; chief among these are the availability of the practical means for action, the political feasibility of such action and the amenability of the national security culture.

Governments express their country's level of ambition in a variety of ways in their security- and defence-policy documents. Levels of transparency and precision about what armed forces are expected to be able to do, how often, for how long, where and under what circumstances vary from state to state. Naturally, national ambition levels are political, subject to shifting priorities and changing policies. And while it has become the norm for EU member states to participate in international crisis-management operations, the precise degree of participation is a subject for intense debate in most contributing states. At the same time, though there is undeniably some volatility in decision-making, national levels of ambition are not simply expressions of political intent at a given point, but are also based on complex defence reviews and form part of long-term planning assumptions. In some countries, they are even used to justify and guide multi-year military reform processes.

It is important to remember that a country's level of ambition is the *maximum* it expects to contribute to military operations other than pure defence operations. It should not be thought to denote the level of engagement that a state seeks to maintain permanently. Most of the time, operational records show missions scoring lower on key indicators such as deployed troops than national levels of ambition specify. As it would be unreasonable to expect states to operate at the maximum level of their ambition most of the time, such discrepancies do not necessarily indicate the presence of a problematic shortfall.

An important measure of a country's level of ambition for international crisis management is of course the quantity of forces that it makes available for deployments. One difficulty is that the deadlines by which a country is expected to meet its stated ambitions are often quite far ahead, and thus there can be a tendency for ambitions to have a rather aspirational character. Given that levels of ambition are key to the long-term planning of acquisitions and force restructuring, this is hardly surprising, but it needs to be borne in mind when comparing states' levels of ambition, as some countries declare their ambition in terms of what they are ready to contribute now, potentially skewing the comparison. For those countries whose ambition levels are set for the future, the level of ambition may relate to a projected future operational strength defined in national planning assumptions, rather than to current capabilities. Nevertheless, even with these qualifications in mind, the contrast between states' ambitions is striking, with those member states located at the upper end of the ambition spectrum aiming to deploy multiples of the percentages of national active forces offered by those at the lower end.

To be a precise guide to what a nation seeks to contribute, the level of ambition needs to include planning assumptions about the concurrency of missions, the sustainability of deployments and the spectrum of tasks to be covered. Some governments qualify their troop commitments by setting limits on the number of missions they will get involved in simultaneously and on how long they will sustain the missions they undertake. Some make a distinction between what they will make available for short-term deployments (i.e., those not involving the rotation of troops) and what they will contribute to deployments that are to be sustained for at least a year. Some governments divide their commitments into troops available for low-, medium- and high-intensity missions, or explicitly limit their ambitions to low- and medium-intensity missions. Among EU members, only seven have precisely expressed levels of ambition on the terms described above.

In 2005, the **Czech Republic** defined its level of ambition for crisis management as participation in a peace-support operation with a mechanised battalion and a special company (up to 1,000 personnel in total), sustainable for a year with rotation at six months, plus deployment of another contingent of 250 personnel for six months without rotation on a humanitarian or rescue mission. It also offered an alternative contribution, whereby the armed forces should be able to deploy one brigade-sized army task force (up to 3,000 personnel) for six months and an equivalent air-force contingent for three months. These numbers work out to 11.5% of active forces for the short-term deployments and 4.8% for the deployments to be sustainable for at least one year. In addition, the Czech army is available to support the Czech police with up to 1,000 personnel for three months and Czech rescue services with up to 1,200 personnel for one month if needed.[7]

In **Estonia**, the level of ambition, to be attainable by 2010, was defined in 2005 as a 'sustainable' (i.e., sustainable for a year or longer) deployment of one infantry company, a Special-Forces platoon, several military observers, a staff element and two vessels. By 2008, up to 250 personnel and one mine-countermeasures vessel were to be available for long-term deployment, the personnel figure rising to 350 by 2010. The maximum number of Estonian troops available for short-term deployment is 850, 20.7% of active forces. Regarding concurrency, Estonia aims to be able to send a contingent on a short-term mission while maintaining one sustainable deployment.[8]

The **French** armed forces have been continuously committed to a wide range of missions worldwide, with an emphasis on peace enforcement and crisis management in Africa, since before the ESDP was created. When announcing the end of conscription in 1996, then-President Jacques Chirac outlined an ambition to be able to send 30,000 personnel abroad for one year to various international theatres, while simultaneously maintaining the capability to send 5,000 troops to smaller theatres. The 2003–08 Military Programme Bill of Law describes the level of ambition for international operations laid out in Chirac's '2015 Armed Forces Model': up to 20,000 land-force personnel are to be available for an unlimited period of time, possibly dispersed across several theatres. For deployments of one year or less, this number could reach 26,000. In addition, the French navy must be able to contribute naval-aviation units plus support, an amphibious task group of 1,400 personnel and nuclear attack submarines. The air force should be able to provide 100 fighter jets and must be able to airlift 15,000 troops across a distance of 5,000km within three days. Up to 600 gendarmes are to be available for international deployment.[9] The White Paper launched by the Sarkozy government in 2008 specified that up to 30,000 ground troops in total would be available for deployments, indicating a slight lowering of targets from previous levels.[10]

Germany's national level of ambition is defined as the ability to sustainably deploy up to 14,000 troops distributed over five areas of operation by the time current reforms have been completed in 2010. An initial force of up to 18,000 troops is earmarked for EU-led missions (including battlegroups). Germany will also make up to 5,000 troops available for NATO Response Force rotations. The country has additionally pledged maritime-patrol aircraft, mine-countermeasures units and 1,000 personnel (including transport and medical personnel, military police and engineers) to the UN Standby Arrangements System.[11] It also reserves another 1,000 soldiers at high readiness for national evacuation and rescue tasks.[12] Adding these numbers up gives a theoretical maximum short-term deployment of 25,000 German troops, or just under 10% of the country's active force.

From 2015 on, **Romania** aims to make available either one division with one combat brigade for six months without rotation; or two combat brigades in either the same or separate operations for six months without rotation; or three battalions in either the same or separate operations for up to 12 months, with rotation after six months.[13] Assuming, then, a maximum short-term contribution of 6,000 troops (two brigades) and a maximum sustainable deployment of up to 3,000 troops, Romania's levels of ambition amount to 8.0% and 4.0% of the active force planned for 2015.

Slovenia seeks to have the capability to sustain one long-term, medium-scale operation at company level and one long-term, small-scale operation at platoon level until 2010. Between 2010 and 2015, the Slovenian government aims to be able to commit one company-level unit to two medium-scale operations for a long-term period and one platoon-level unit to a long-term, small-scale operation. Alternatively, a battalion-sized unit could be deployed to a large-scale operation for up to six months. From 2015, the commitment of one company to two long-term, medium-scale operations and one platoon to one long-term, small-scale operation is planned, or alternatively one battalion to one large-scale operation for up to 12 months.[14]

The **United Kingdom** expresses its level of ambition in the form of three concurrency suites based on different assumptions about the number of operations, the scale of effort involved and the duration of the operations. The standard configuration ('Suite A') would allow for one sustainable medium-scale operation, a simultaneous sustainable small-scale operation and one one-off (without rotation) small-scale intervention. Alternatively, the sustainable medium-scale operation could be undertaken at the same time as a sustainable small-scale operation, plus a limited-duration, medium-scale intervention ('Suite B'). With some lead time, UK forces would be prepared to conduct a demanding one-off, large-scale operation while simultaneously staying engaged in a small-scale peace-support operation ('Suite C'). In all three cases, permanent commitments to quick-reaction forces would be maintained.[15]

The UK Ministry of Defence does not express its concurrency suites in terms of manpower but in terms of the number of units necessary to conduct the operation. However, by referring to the force structure outlined in ministry documents,[16] it is possible to calculate that the large-scale operation in Suite C would involve some 40,000 land forces, plus air and naval elements. The small-scale peace-support operation would involve around 2,300 land forces. The numbers for land forces in Suite A are estimated at 8,000 for the sustainable medium-scale operation, 3,000 for the sustainable small-scale operation and 4,000 for the small-scale intervention; for Suite B, the sustainable medium-scale operation and sustainable small-scale operation would be the same size as in suite A, while the medium-scale intervention would involve some 16,500 land forces. It is further assumed that, in order to be able to sustain extended deployments involving the rotation of forces, it would be necessary for the armed forces to have available three or four times the number of ships and five times the number of army and air-force units and crews as would actually be deployed.

There are a further three EU countries that have also defined their ambitions for sustainability and concurrency of operations but have not fully specified both maximum short-term and long-term deployment numbers. In **Austria**, the level of ambition has been defined as two battalions plus support forces for unlimited deployment on stabilisation and reconstruction missions of low to medium intensity. In addition, a 'framework' brigade (i.e., a brigade designed to lead a multinational force) at 30-day readiness, sustainable for one year, is planned for high-intensity missions such as Separation of Parties by Force, and the Austrian government also aims to develop the ability to maintain a classic peacekeeping deployment comparable to its commitment in the Golan Heights. Thus, the number of Austrian troops sustainable for at least 12 months is expected to be some 4,400 by 2012. For low- and medium-intensity missions, deployments would not be limited to 12 months. If its reform plans are implemented in their entirety, Austria's short-term contribution to EU missions could reach 3,500 troops.[17]

Lithuania's goal is to deploy larger, self-sustaining units, while simultaneously reducing the number of missions in which Lithuanian forces are involved. From 2015, a 950-strong battalion task force, including combat support and combat service support, plus a 50-strong Special-Forces squadron, is to be sustainable with full rotation in one operation. As an alternative, Lithuania also aims to make available three specialist units, each of company strength, for simultaneous deployment. The country aims to be able to participate in up to three international deployments in addition to up to two domestic-assistance missions.[18]

The level of ambition of the **Netherlands**, confirmed in 2007, is a deployment at brigade level with two squadrons of fighter jets or a maritime task force on high-intensity missions sustainable for up to one year. In addition, the country also aims to be able to provide three battalion-sized task groups (or their air and naval equivalents) for low-intensity missions over a prolonged period of time. In 2007, at least 5,000 troops, or 11% of active forces, were available for deployments of at least one year's duration. Special-operations personnel are also available for evacuation and counter-terrorism purposes. The Netherlands intends to be able to function as a lead nation at brigade level and, in conjunction with other countries, at corps level in land operations.[19]

Less than half of the EU's member states have a closely defined level of ambition for international crisis-management missions. However, it is possible to glean at least the basic parameters of most countries' ambitions from publicly available documents. Table 4 overleaf summarises what is known for all 27 member states.

Operational record

Countries' operational records can be expressed in similar terms to their levels of ambition: the quantity of forces deployed on international crisis-management missions (and the proportion of the country's total active forces this represents); the number of missions simultaneously engaged in; the sustainability of the deployments undertaken; and the intensity of the operations participated in.

Between 2003 and 2007, the EU as a whole sustained between 60,000 and 70,000 personnel on international crisis-management missions. The proportion of member states' armed forces that was deployed in such missions varied widely. Over the five-year period, of the 25 member states that had troops deployed, only the UK managed an average of more than 7% of active forces. A further six countries – Denmark, France, Ireland, Italy, Luxembourg and the Netherlands – deployed an average of 4% to 6.9%. The remaining 18 member states deployed on average less than 4% of their active forces, with the EU average for this period being 3.5% of active forces. A group of six countries beat the EU average every year: Denmark, France, Ireland, Luxembourg (which of course makes a small contribution in absolute terms), the Netherlands and the UK. Cyprus and Malta had no troops deployed. Eleven countries among the 25 contributing nations failed to beat the average even once, among them Germany, Poland and Spain.[20] Table 5 shows the deployment figures for each country.

Table 4: EU member states' levels of ambition for deployment to international crisis-management operations

Country	Max. short-term deployment/% of active forces	Sustainable for at least 1 year/% of active forces	Concurrency assumptions	Sustainability assumptions	ESDP task spectrum covered?	Timescale
Austria	Not known	4,400 (11.1%)	At least two simultaneous deployments	Continuous deployment for low- and medium-intensity missions, up to one year for high-intensity missions	Yes	By 2012
Belgium	Not known	Not known	Not known	Not known	Yes	Unclear
Bulgaria	4,500 (11%)	Not known	Not known	Not known	Yes	By 2015
Cyprus	Niche contributions	Niche contributions	Not known	Not known	No combat forces	Current
Czech Republic	3,000 (11.5%)	1,250 (4.8%)	Two international deployments at maximum troop levels plus domestic civilian-assistance mission	One year	Yes	Current
Denmark	5,000 (16.7%)	2,000 (6.7%)	Not known	Continuous deployment	Yes	By 2009
Estonia	850 (20.7%)	350 (8.5%)	One long-term deployment plus one short-term deployment	Sustainable, but unclear duration	Yes	By 2010
Finland	Not known	1,000 (3.4%)	Not known	Not known	Yes	Current
France	30,000 (13.4%)	20,000 (8.9%)	Dispersed deployments across several theatres simultaneously	Continuous deployment	Yes	By 2015
Germany	25,000 (9.9%)	14,000 (5.5%)	Five areas of simultaneous operation	Continuous deployment	Yes	By 2010
Greece	Not known	3,550 (2.5%)	Not known	Not known	Yes	Current
Hungary	Not known	1,600 (5.7%)	Not known	Sustainable, but unclear duration	Yes	By 2010
Ireland	1,600 (15.2%)	850 (8.1%)	Simultaneous deployments, details not clear	Continuous deployment	Yes	By 2010
Italy	Not known	13,000 (8.1%)	Simultaneous deployments, details not clear	Continuous deployment	Yes	By 2019

Table 4: EU member states' levels of ambition for deployment to international crisis-management operations (cont.)

Country	Max. short-term deployment/% of active forces	Sustainable for at least 1 year/% of active forces	Concurrency assumptions	Sustainability assumptions	ESDP task spectrum covered?	Timescale
Latvia	Not known	1,000 (10%)	Three to four simultaneous deployments	Continuous deployment	Yes	By 2012
Lithuania	Not known	1,000 (9.4%)	Up to three simultaneous international deployments plus up to two domestic- assistance missions	Continuous deployment	Yes	By 2015
Luxemb.	Niche contributions	Niche contributions	Not known	Not known	Yes	Unclear
Malta	Niche contributions	Niche contributions	Not known	Not known	Not known	Current
Nether.	Not known	5,000 (11%)	Simultaneous deployments but details not clear	One year	Yes	Current
Poland	Not known	4,000 (3.1%)	Simultaneous deployments but details not clear	Sustainable, but unclear duration	Yes	Current
Portugal	Not known	1,500 (3.5%)	Not known	Not known	Yes	Current
Romania	6,000 (8%)	3,000 (4%)	Up to three simultaneous deployments	One year	Yes	By 2015
Slovakia	Not known	1,150 (6.4%)	Simultaneous deployments but details not clear	Continuous deployment at company level	Yes	By 2015
Slovenia	1,400 (16.5%)	500 (5.9%)	Up to three simultaneous deployments	Up to one year for battalion level or continuous deployment at company level	Yes	By 2015
Spain	Not known	6,000 (4.3%)	Simultaneous deployments but details not clear	Continuous deployment	Yes	By 2015
Sweden	2,300 (9.6%)	Not known	Up to five simultaneous deployments	Not known	Yes	Current
United Kingdom	55,000 (30.5%)	25,000 (13.9%)	Three 'concurrency suites' with different combinations of simultaneous missions	Continuous deployment	Yes	Current

Sources: see[21]

Table 5: **Deployments (incl. observers) of EU member states, 2003–2007**

	2003		2004		2005		2006		2007		Average
	No.	% active forces	No.	% active forces	No.	% active forces	No.	% active forces	No.	% active forces	% active forces
Austria	933	2.70	922	2.63	1,217	3.05	1,230	3.11	1,118	2.82	2.86
Belgium	683	1.67	768	1.88	785	2.12	1,118	2.82	1,279	3.22	2.34
Bulgaria	543	1.06	546	1.07	554	1.09	654	1.28	719	1.76	1.25
Czech R.	1,219	2.14	562	1.25	729	3.27	899	3.63	1,089	4.71	3.00
Denmark	1,543	6.74	920	4.34	1,108	5.23	1,366	6.32	1,409	6.22	5.77
Estonia	3	0.05	153	3.07	65	1.32	221	5.39	201	4.78	2.92
Finland	917	3.40	1,083	4.01	762	2.69	779	2.66	895	3.05	3.16
France	11,025	4.26	10,483	4.05	9,733	3.82	11,766	4.62	11,497	4.51	4.25
Germany	6,810	2.39	7,203	2.53	7,142	2.51	9,008	3.67	7,045	2.89	2.80
Greece	1,989	1.12	2,085	1.22	1,590	0.97	1,992	1.35	1,165	0.74	1.08
Hungary	1,039	3.11	1,049	3.25	1,224	3.79	705	2.18	1,010	3.12	3.09
Ireland	443	4.24	633	6.05	722	6.90	660	6.30	847	8.13	6.32
Italy	9,537	4.77	7,868	4.06	8,159	4.27	6,482	3.39	7,717	4.16	4.13
Latvia	165	3.38	103	2.11	161	3.07	165	3.09	119	2.10	2.75
Lithuania	174	1.37	223	1.65	214	1.58	222	1.85	236	1.70	1.63
Luxemb.	60	6.67	58	6.44	55	6.11	39	4.33	35	5.00	5.71
Netherl.	2,792	5.26	2,265	4.26	2,246	4.23	2,400	4.52	1,871	4.10	4.47
Poland	3,856	2.37	3,887	2.75	2,113	1.49	4,246	3.00	3,555	2.79	2.48
Portugal	1,438	3.20	1,294	2.88	715	1.59	795	1.81	680	1.58	2.21
Romania	1,569	1.61	1,558	1.60	2,137	2.20	1,578	2.27	1,403	2.02	1.94
Slovakia	852	3.87	769	3.81	569	2.82	633	4.16	530	3.09	3.55
Slovenia	85	1.30	180	2.75	245	3.74	312	4.76	198	3.31	3.17
Spain	4,158	2.76	2,270	1.51	2,439	1.66	3,400	2.31	2,762	1.85	2.02
Sweden	779	2.82	1,034	3.75	941	3.41	834	3.02	996	4.15	3.43
UK	17,669	8.31	11,553	5.56	14,421	6.65	16,509	8.64	14,883	8.24	7.48
Total	70,281	3.51	59,469	3.06	60,046	3.13	68,013	3.77	63,359	4.02	3.50

Note: Precise figures on troop deployments over time for all countries are difficult to obtain. The number of deployed personnel varies from month to month. The numbers presented here are a best estimate based on data available to the IISS *Military Balance*, which publishes an annual 'snapshot' of troops deployed and does not seek to pinpoint an average of troops deployed during a year. Short-term operational deployments may be missed, and the use of Special Forces is often not made public. For example, the UK deployed 45,000 personnel, including 26,000 ground troops, for the invasion of Iraq in 2003. Figures cited here include multinational operations and operations conducted by individual countries arising from bilateral defence agreements or upon invitation by a host government. They do not include permanent military bases (this is particularly relevant for France and the UK, both of which have significant troop numbers based in third countries).

Source: IISS.

As it is safe to assume that demand for crisis management will continue to come from a variety of different sources at once, EU member states need to be able to make simultaneous deployments. However, a snapshot of 2007 reveals similar disparities in performance on concurrency as on troop quantities. On the face of it, member states might appear to be doing well on concurrency. All 25 countries that had troops deployed that year engaged in at least four missions. Of those, 14 countries were committed to ten or more simultaneously, with France being involved in no fewer than 20 missions. But though there were 263 national contingents deployed in 2007, almost 70% of those contingents were made up of fewer than 100 soldiers, and many amounted to little more than a handful of troops. The majority of EU member states appear unable to deploy formations of even battalion size (500–800 troops) on a single mission. In 2007, only Austria, the Czech Republic, France, Germany, Greece, Italy, the Netherlands, Poland, Romania, Spain and the UK managed to contribute a battalion-sized or larger contingent to one mission. Only the three largest EU members – France, Germany and the UK – deployed at least one brigade-sized (3,000–5,000 troops) formation to a single mission. The UK contingent in Afghanistan, then around 7,400 strong, was the largest national contingent deployed on a crisis-management mission.[22] Most states concentrate the bulk of their deployed troops in one or two missions, resulting in a high number of token contributions to many others. This can result in the kinds of problems associated with heavily multinational missions discussed in the previous chapter, including command-and-control difficulties arising from the presence of contingents too small to be employed as discrete units. Figure 1 overleaf shows the total number of missions each troop-contributing EU country was involved in in 2007 alongside the number of missions in which national contingents of at least 100 troops (roughly a company) were involved. The latter deployments generally tally with states' levels of ambition for concurrency.

Sustainability too is crucial: while some missions do require rapid but brief deployments, by and large contemporary crisis-management missions tend to be of significant length. Hence, states need to be able to sustain contributions beyond the standard six-month tour in theatre. Encouragingly, long-term data suggests that once EU member states start contributing to international crisis-management missions, they do not stop. In general, the percentages of active forces deployed do not oscillate substantially, meaning that contributions are by and large sustainable. But, as we have seen, national forces are sustained at very different levels. Greece, for example, demonstrates the comparatively low importance it

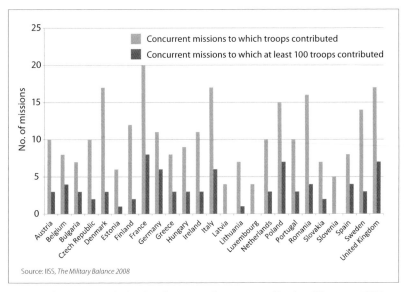

Source: IISS, *The Military Balance 2008*

Figure 1: **Concurrent mission involvement of troop-contributing EU states, 2007**

attaches to international crisis management by continuously deploying only around 1% of its active forces. France, on the other hand, maintains a contribution level of 4% to 4.5%, and Ireland usually deploys more than 6%.[23]

In some countries, such as Belgium, there has been an increase in the percentage contributed over the past five years, while in a few others, such as Portugal, performance has worsened. Others, such as Slovenia, have significantly expanded their contributions in recent years but now appear to have plateaued, at least for the time being. Estonia is one of the few countries in which there are significant swings, with a year of relatively high deployment levels followed by a marked drop, but its overall trajectory is upward.[24]

The deployment levels of some of the most engaged countries, such as Denmark and the UK, also show significant variation. However, even at their lowest levels these states still deploy a higher percentage of their active forces than do most other EU members. In the case of the UK, it is worth noting that British deployment figures are always highest at the beginnings of missions or at points of heightened crisis, for example in Kosovo in 1999, in Afghanistan in 2001–02 and since 2007, and in Iraq in 2003. In other words, the UK not only deploys a high percentage of its forces but it also deploys it in the most difficult situations, in which rapid reaction is needed and the security environment is volatile or

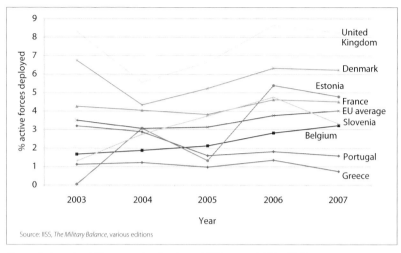

Source: IISS, *The Military Balance*, various editions

Figure 2: **Sustainability records of selected EU states, 2003–2007**

outright hostile. A selection of states' sustainability records is displayed in Figure 2.

The overall operational record of EU member states on the various types of mission is largely positive. Table 6 below shows that in crisis-management operations initiated between 1995 and 2007, member states covered all of the ESDP's illustrative scenarios, including those at the upper end of the intensity spectrum. Twenty of the EU's 27 members have participated in a mission that (although not within the ESDP framework) can broadly be described as a Separation of Parties by Force scenario, either in *Operation Allied Force* in the former Yugoslavia in 1999 or in *Operation Iraqi Freedom* in Iraq in 2003[25] (it should be remembered that Separation of Parties by Force missions are not restricted to the scenario described in the title, but cover a range of crisis-management tasks for combat forces[26]). However, the roles played by individual countries in these missions varied greatly, as the debate on national restrictions on troop activities, or 'caveats', shows. Thus, in practice, not all countries have participated fully in types of mission at the higher end of the task spectrum.

Governments often place restrictions on the activities of forces deployed on international missions. This is partly to ensure that forces are not used by commanders to undertake activities for which they are not trained or equipped. In practice, however, caveats are also used to ensure that forces do not participate in activities that might be controversial at home.

For security reasons, the details of national caveats are not usually published. However, much is known about how caveats have been used in recent years. There have been restrictions on where troops can be used – for example, countries have imposed caveats preventing movement of their troops to regions where fighting is particularly intense. The forces of some countries are not allowed to initiate combat operations. Some contingents have been allowed to operate only during daylight. More specific examples of caveats include a state's transport aircraft not being allowed to land on gravel strips, significantly reducing their usability in some theatres. In some cases, aircraft have been prevented from flying at night. In others, patrols have been permitted only in armoured vehicles and only when a certain combination of vehicles has been available. Some countries reserve several days to decide whether to allow units to deploy beyond their area of operations, preventing a rapid response to operational needs.

Despite ongoing tensions over the issue of caveats, there is evidence that a common understanding on the issue is gradually emerging. In Kosovo, most caveats relating to NATO forces were eventually abandoned after proving unworkable. When civil unrest broke out there in 2004, many units were not allowed to use their firearms unless their lives were in danger. But positions began to shift as the difficulty of operating under such restrictions became clear, with Slovenia specifically removing its firearms caveat when it increased its presence in the NATO-led peacekeeping force KFOR in 2007.[27] In 2006, General James Jones, then-NATO Supreme Allied Commander, remarked that, in 2004, KFOR 'had so many caveats that our commanders spent more time trying to figure out what they couldn't do with their forces than what they could do. Today ... we have very few caveats [in Kosovo]'.[28]

In Afghanistan, a number of caveats relating to the NATO-led International Security Assistance Force (ISAF) forces were removed following NATO's Riga Summit in 2006. Before the summit, only six NATO members had no caveats in place in relation to ISAF.[29] There were at least 50 caveats with operational impact, and the total number of restrictions reportedly topped 100.[30] At Riga, France and Germany agreed to remove some of their restrictions. Other countries, including the Czech Republic, Denmark, Greece, Hungary, Lithuania, the Netherlands, Romania and Slovenia, removed all or almost all of their caveats. NATO Secretary-General Jaap de Hoop Scheffer remarked at the time that: 'About 26,000 of the total 32,000 NATO ISAF forces are now more useable than they were'.[31] Nonetheless, General Dan McNeill, ISAF commander in 2007 and 2008, has said that he has been frustrated by the degree to which caveats 'impinge on my ability to properly plan, resource and prosecute effective military operations',[32] indicating that this problem that has plagued many commanders before him has not yet gone away.

While caveats are usually declared at the point at which forces are made available, national-contingent commanders are always able to prevent their forces from being used if they feel the intended use goes against the instructions of their political overseers. These so-called 'undeclared caveats' are particularly damaging because they are hidden until the moment a particular problem arises.

Whether official or undeclared, caveats undoubtedly impede commanders' operational flexibility and effectiveness. However, their effect is two-sided. In many cases, caveats have effectively enabled deployments to be made, by making it easier for national politicians to muster domestic support for an intervention. As a result, more countries are able to participate in multinational operations, thus increasing the political legitimacy of these operations, both domestically and internationally.

The politics behind caveats are well understood, and generally accepted. Former Commander of ISAF General David Richards has wryly remarked that he 'now know[s] more about the politics of the ... 26 nations of NATO than [he] ever thought [he] would'.[33] UK Defence Secretary Des Browne has observed that 'caveats are a matter of political choice ... The political circumstances of countries are different and an appreciation of those circumstances sometimes helps one to understand why there are some limits on what they agree to do'.[34] The challenge is to minimise caveats that are operationally harmful while allowing for those that are politically necessary. As Afghanistan has demonstrated, this may not always be possible, and arguments about burden-sharing can become very divisive. The remark made in 2006 by Radek Sikorski, then-Polish defence minister, that 'Those who give without caveats are giving twice as much' shows the resentment the issue can engender among allies.[35] But caveats represent a compromise between legitimacy and effectiveness, and they cannot be avoided if operations are to involve the cooperation of a wide range of countries with differing views about the use of armed force.

Scorecard

Having surveyed national levels of ambition and the broad outline of each country's operational record, is it now possible to draw more precise conclusions about European ambitions and achievements in this field? Clearly, an exact measurement of a country's performance in terms of its operational record and declared ambitions is not practicable (at least not without access to classified information), and could in any case be misunderstood as an

Table 6: Military crisis-management operations involving EU states initiated 1995–2007

Mission	Framework and duration	Type of mission (EU scenario)	Contributing EU members
Croatia (UNCRO/UNTAES)	UN, 1995–1997	Stabilisation and Reconstruction	Belgium, Czech R., Denmark, Estonia, Finland, France, Ireland, Lithuania, Netherlands, Poland, Portugal, Slovakia, Spain, Sweden, UK
Macedonia (UNPREDEP)	UN, 1995–1998	Stabilisation and Reconstruction	Belgium, Czech R., Denmark, Finland, France, Ireland, Poland, Portugal, Spain, Sweden
Bosnia (IFOR/SFOR)	NATO, 1997–2003	Stabilisation and Reconstruction	Austria, Belgium, Bulgaria, Czech R., Denmark, Estonia, Finland, France, Germany, Greece, Hungary, Ireland, Italy, Latvia, Lithuania, Luxembourg, Netherlands, Poland, Portugal, Romania, Slovakia, Slovenia, Spain, Sweden, UK
Albania (ALBA)	Coalition, 1997	Conflict Prevention	Austria, Denmark, France, Greece, Italy, Romania, Spain
Albania (AFOR)	NATO, 1999	Humanitarian Assistance	Austria, Belgium, Denmark, France, Germany, Greece, Italy, Lithuania, Netherlands, Poland, Romania, Slovakia, Spain, UK
Kosovo (Allied Force)	NATO, 1999	Separation of Parties by Force	Belgium, Czech R., Denmark, France, Germany, Greece, Hungary, Italy, Luxembourg, Netherlands, Poland, Portugal, Spain, UK
Kosovo (KFOR)	NATO, since 1999	Stabilisation and Reconstruction	Austria, Belgium, Bulgaria, Czech R., Denmark, Estonia, Finland, France, Germany, Greece, Hungary, Ireland, Italy, Latvia, Lithuania, Luxembourg, Netherlands, Poland, Portugal, Romania, Slovakia, Slovenia, Spain, Sweden, UK
Sierra Leone (UNAMSIL)	UN, 1999–2005	Stabilisation and Reconstruction	Denmark, Czech R., France, Germany, Slovakia, Sweden, UK
Sierra Leone (Palliser)	UK, 2000–2002	Evacuation, then Stabilisation and Reconstruction	UK
Macedonia (Essential Harvest/ Amber Fox)	NATO, 2001–2003	Conflict Prevention	Belgium, Czech R., Denmark, France, Germany, Greece, Hungary, Italy, Netherlands, Poland, Portugal, Spain, UK
Mediterranean (Active Endeavour)	NATO, since 2001	Conflict Prevention	Belgium, Denmark, Germany, Greece, Italy, Netherlands, Poland, Portugal, Spain, UK
Various areas (Enduring Freedom)	Coalition, since 2001	Stabilisation and Reconstruction	Czech R., Denmark, France, Germany, Italy, Netherlands, Poland, Romania, Slovakia, Spain

(cont.)

Table 6: Military crisis-management operations involving EU states initiated 1995–2007 (cont.)

Mission	Framework and duration	Type of mission (EU scenario)	Contributing EU members
Afghanistan (ISAF)	Coalition from 2001, then NATO since 2003	Stabilisation and Reconstruction	Austria, Belgium, Bulgaria, Czech R., Denmark, Estonia, Finland, France, Germany, Greece, Hungary, Ireland, Italy, Latvia, Lithuania, Luxembourg, Netherlands, Poland, Portugal, Romania, Slovakia, Slovenia, Spain, Sweden, UK
Timor Leste (UNMISET)	UN, 2002–2005	Stabilisation and Reconstruction	Denmark, Portugal, Slovakia, Sweden
Côte d'Ivoire (Licorne)	France, since 2002	Separation of Parties by Force, then Stabilisation and Reconstruction	France
Iraq (Iraqi Freedom)	Coalition, since 2003	Warfare, then Stabilisation and Reconstruction	Bulgaria, Czech R., Denmark, Estonia, Hungary, Italy, Latvia, Lithuania, Netherlands, Poland, Portugal, Romania, Slovakia, Spain, UK
DRC (Artemis)	EU, 2003	Conflict Prevention	Austria, Belgium, France, Germany, Greece, Hungary, Ireland, Italy, Netherlands, Spain, Sweden, UK
Liberia (UNMIL)	UN, since 2003	Stabilisation and Reconstruction	Bulgaria, Czech R., Denmark, Finland, France, Germany, Ireland, Poland, Romania, Sweden, UK
Bosnia (EUFOR/Althea)	EU, since 2004	Stabilisation and Reconstruction	Austria, Belgium, Bulgaria, Czech R., Denmark, Estonia, Finland, France, Germany, Greece, Hungary, Ireland, Italy, Latvia, Lithuania, Luxembourg, Netherlands, Poland, Portugal, Romania, Slovakia, Slovenia, Spain, Sweden, UK
DRC (EUFOR RD Congo)	EU, 2006	Conflict Prevention	Austria, Belgium, Czech R., Finland, France, Germany, Greece, Hungary, Ireland, Italy, Lithuania, Luxembourg, Netherlands, Poland, Portugal, Slovakia, Slovenia, Spain, Sweden, UK
Lebanon (UNIFIL II)	UN, since 2006	Stabilisation and Reconstruction	Belgium, Bulgaria, Denmark, Finland, France, Germany, Greece, Hungary, Ireland, Italy, Luxembourg, Netherlands, Poland, Portugal, Spain
Chad/Central African Republic (EUFOR Chad/CAR)	EU, since 2008	Stabilisation and Reconstruction	Austria, Belgium, Bulgaria, Cyprus, Czech R., Finland, France, Germany, Greece, Hungary, Ireland, Italy, Lithuania, Luxembourg, Netherlands, Poland, Portugal, Romania, Slovakia, Slovenia, Spain, Sweden, UK

Source: IISS

This table includes only those operations that have had at least 500 European troops deployed at any one time since initiation of the mission.

exercise in ranking countries. But it should be both possible and useful to map the diversity of commitment that exists among EU member states using generic categories such as 'high', 'medium' and 'low'.

A state's commitment to crisis-management operations is expressed in its level of ambition for participation in such missions and in its actual performance in them. Performance and ambition can both be measured in terms of the four major indicators discussed above. *Numbers* are shown by the percentage of active forces deployed (performance) and made available for deployments (ambition); *concurrency* is seen in the number of simultaneous operations engaged in (performance) and planned for (ambition); *sustainability* can be seen in the duration of deployments (performance) and in planning assumptions about duration (ambition); and *levels of mission intensity* are shown by the types of mission a country has participated in in the past (performance) and is prepared to participate in in the future (ambition). A full analysis of a state's commitment according to these four indicators gives us its crisis-management profile. Assessments of ambition levels need to take into account the detail in which ambitions are defined, as well as how demanding the aspirations are. As reasonably detailed data on ambition levels is only available in open sources for ten of the 25 troop-contributing member states, it is only possible to draw up a full crisis-management profile for those ten. Nevertheless, it is still possible to broadly assess the bulk of states in terms of their performance and ambition.

Ambition

A rough scoring system, outlined below, can be applied to the ambition levels of the ten states for which sufficient data is available in each of the four main categories.

Numbers pledged

Countries declaring an ambition to provide a sustainable deployment that represents a proportion of their active forces that is at least twice the average proportion pledged for the period 2003–2007 (3.5%), i.e., 7.0% or more of active forces, receive a score of three for this indicator. Countries that plan for sustainable deployments of 5%–6.8% receive a score of two, those planning to sustain 3%–4.9% a score of one and the rest a score of nought. Regarding the precision with which ambitions are defined, one point will be awarded for ambitions that relate to existing, rather than projected, capabilities and a further point will be given if both a maximum short-term deployment and a maximum sustainable deployment are defined. The highest possible score for this indicator is therefore five.

Concurrency

Those countries whose levels of ambition make explicit assumptions about concurrency will receive a score of one, while those that do not will receive a score of nought. Any country that plans to sustain three or more missions simultaneously receives another point. The maximum possible score is thus two.

Sustainability

If a country's level of ambition includes provision for sustainable missions, the country receives a score of one; if not, its score is nought.

Intensity of missions

All EU member states (except for Denmark, which has an opt-out) participate in the ESDP. As a result, almost all member states subscribe to the task spectrum covered by the policy, which includes combat operations in crisis management (and Denmark too is prepared to undertake such missions in alternative frameworks, such as NATO or coalitions). Only Cyprus has explicitly declared that it will not contribute combat forces to crisis management, at least not for the time being. This could lead us to the conclusion that all EU states apart from Cyprus should be marked up on this count. However, since the ESDP task spectrum was agreed by all EU governments and could thus be interpreted as underpinning the entire notion of national ambitions, awarding on this basis would seem largely redundant. Thus, no scores will be given for ambition in this category.

States can therefore attain a maximum score of eight for ambition. Those scoring seven or eight are classed as having a high level of ambition, those scoring between four and six a medium level and those with a score of three or less a low level. Of the ten countries for which scores can be assigned, France and the UK fall into the 'high' category and all the remaining countries (Austria, the Czech Republic, Estonia, Germany, Lithuania, the Netherlands, Romania and Slovenia) are located in the 'medium' category.

Performance

In contrast to ambition levels, on performance, enough data exists for each of the 25 troop-contributing EU member states to be scored.

Numbers deployed

For every year between 2003 and 2007 that a country beats the EU average for the proportion of active forces deployed on crisis-management missions it receives one point. In addition, countries that deploy an average of 6% of national forces or more receive three points, those deploying 4%–5.9% receive two, those deploying 2%–3.9% receive one and those that deploy less than 2% receive nought. Thus, a total of eight points may be awarded for this category.

Concurrency

In view of the fact that many of the contingents that are contributed to crisis-management operations are very small, the simple number of missions a country is involved in is not in itself a meaningful measure of its success on concurrency. Thus, only simultaneous contributions of a minimum of 100 troops, or roughly a company, will be counted as concurrent missions for the purposes of this assessment. EU member states that deployed four or more company-sized contingents in 2007 will receive a score of two, those that contributed two or three will receive a score of one and all others will receive a score of nought.

Sustainability

All EU member states except for Cyprus and Malta contribute at least some troops to crisis-management missions year after year. The most useful indicator of the sustainability of a state's contributions, therefore, is whether these contributions rise and fall broadly in line with the overall EU trend. For example, if the total number of troops deployed by member states increased over a period of time but a particular state's contribution decreased over the same period, this would show either that that country was unable to keep up with demand or that it was simply not responsive to it. So countries that moved in sync with the overall trend each year between 2003 and 2007 receive a score of two, those that moved against the trend in no more than one year in the period receive a score of one and those that moved against the trend in more than one year receive nought. (If a country were to raise its deployment level from one year to the next in a period in which the wider trend was downward, that country should not of course be penalised by any scoring system for breaking that trend.)

Intensity of types of mission

Those countries that have participated at least once in each of the five types of mission outlined by the ESDP's illustrative scenarios receive a score of two, those that have participated in all operations except for those involving combat receive a score of one and those with a patchier record nought. (As detailed information on national restrictions is

Table 7: **Crisis-management profiles of ten EU states**

Ambition		Low	Medium	High
Performance	Low		Austria Lithuania	
	Medium		Czech Republic Estonia Germany Romania Slovenia	
	High		Netherlands	France United Kingdom

classified, it is not possible to take caveats into consideration in this assessment.)

In total, then, on the performance side, countries can attain a maximum score of 14. (The scale is heavily weighted towards the percentage of troops deployed because personnel shortfalls are one of the key problems facing contemporary crisis management.) Countries scoring between 11 and 14 fall into the 'high performance' category, those attaining between six and ten are 'medium' and those with five points or fewer are 'low performance'. Of the 25 troop-contributing member states, six – Denmark, France, Ireland, Italy, Netherlands and the UK – are high-performance countries. The medium category is populated by 11 member states: Belgium, the Czech Republic, Estonia, Germany, Hungary, Luxembourg, Romania, Slovakia, Slovenia, Spain and Sweden. The remaining eight states – Austria, Bulgaria, Finland, Greece, Latvia, Lithuania, Poland and Portugal – are low-level performers.

Those countries that can be scored on both ambition and performance can be assigned an overall crisis-management profile and grouped accordingly. Table 7 shows the profiles of these ten states.

As the table shows, there are essentially two types of profile. In the first type, ambitions and performance are aligned. Within this type can be found both countries with medium scores (the Czech Republic, Estonia, Germany, Romania and Slovenia) and countries with high scores (France and the UK). In the second profile type, ambitions and performance are at different levels. This is the case for Austria and Lithuania, whose ambitions outrun their current levels of performance, and for the Netherlands, where the opposite is true. Chapter 3 will examine the various factors, domestic and international, that have contributed to the formation of these profiles.

CHAPTER THREE

Domestic Determinants of National Profiles: Constraints or Enablers?

What determines the levels of ambition and the operational record that together make up a state's crisis-management profile? Differences between types of governance and levels of income, development and involvement in international organisations are sometimes offered as explanations for the disparities between states' contributions to international efforts, but these factors cannot explain the high-to-low spread of crisis-management profiles observed in the previous chapter. All ten countries profiled in Chapter 2 are, of course, EU members (although not all are NATO members) and all are stable democracies with high levels of income and development, at least by global standards. All are economically dependent on international trade.

Instead, the three broad domestic factors of the availability of military means, the character of a state's security culture, and the limits placed on its capacity for action abroad by its decision-making institutions and public opinion appear to be the most important influences on a state's action in this field. None of these factors alone explains the outcomes identified above; they are interrelated and develop their explanatory power only in conjunction with each other. The role of these factors in creating the crisis-management profiles of Austria, Germany and the UK – low/medium-, medium- and high-profile countries respectively – are explored further below.

Available means: key capabilities and financial resources

Modern military operations, even low–intensity ones, demand a specific capabilities profile.[1] Contemporary crisis-management missions, which are in principle without geographical limitations, require long-distance transport capabilities ('strategic lift'). As such missions are conducted in multinational frameworks, forces also need to be interoperable. Some missions require rapid-reaction capabilities, while almost all are conducted in pursuit of limited political objectives and require armed forces to cover a wide task spectrum, from combat to police activity to advice-giving, mentoring and diplomacy. Forces must also be deployable with high levels of readiness. Once in theatre, they need to be sustainable and able to react flexibly to the situation on the ground. All this requires particular capabilities and resources, including robust logistical capabilities, deployable command and control, communications, intelligence, surveillance, reconnaissance and target-acquisition systems, precision and stand-off strike capabilities, combat search-and-rescue resources, air-to-air refuelling capacity, deployable air defence, force-protection capabilities, psychological operations and Special-Forces contingents, and a civil–military cooperation capacity. Many defence-reform programmes in EU member states aim to improve capabilities in some or most of these areas,[2] but only a few already possess a full complement of such capabilities.

The revised Petersberg tasks include demanding, high-intensity operations. Though they fall short of expeditionary warfare, these missions do require some expeditionary-warfare capabilities. Clearly, the existence or otherwise of such capabilities in the national inventory is central to whether a country sets its ambitions at the upper end of the Petersberg task spectrum and whether its operational record matches those ambitions. Of the EU member states, only France and the UK possess the assets needed for the highest-intensity missions. Germany is in the process of trying to plug the gaps in its resources on this front. Other European states with the potential to make a significant contribution, including on the more demanding operations, include Italy, the Netherlands and Spain. The remainder of the EU membership will be essentially limited to smaller roles in high-intensity missions – or, perhaps, gradually increasing contributions to medium- and low-intensity missions – for the foreseeable future.

Clearly, a state's access to sophisticated capabilities and its ability to undertake complex operations largely depends on its financial resources. While between them, EU member states spent some €204 billion on defence in 2006,[3] defence expenditure varies widely from state to state, not only in terms of the percentage of GDP allocated but also in how the money is distributed within the defence realm.

Austria has struggled to shift its focus from the traditional low- and medium-intensity peacekeeping operations in which its armed forces have been involved for decades to more demanding operations. It continues to contribute almost exclusively to post-conflict operations.[4] This is mostly a result of capability shortfalls. The Austrian military's procurement activities over the past decade as part of its defence-reform programme have demonstrated an awareness of this problem and some willingness to tackle it.

In 2000, the Austrian government announced the expansion of the helicopter fleet through the acquisition of nine S-70A *Black Hawks,* designed to improve in-theatre tactical transport capabilities. These were delivered in 2002. In 2003, the Austrian air force took over three C-130K transport aircraft from the UK. In addition to 112 *Ulan* armoured personnel carriers acquired between 2002 and 2004, the Austrian Ministry of Defence bought 20 *Dingo* 2 armoured vehicles (which can be transported in C-130K aircraft), delivered in 2005. Some of these were immediately deployed to Afghanistan. An order has been made for 129 *Pandur* II armoured vehicles, though this has yet to be fulfilled. It has also been reported that up to 24,000 body-armour kits have been ordered for the army and that there are plans to invest in new command and communications equipment. Combined reconnaissance artillery battalions have also been set up as part of the defence-reform programme. Finally, Austria is due to take delivery of 15 *Typhoon* fighter aircraft by 2009; the first was delivered in July 2007. For the time being, however, the Austrian *Typhoons* will provide air defence without the IRIS-T missiles they were originally intended to carry, and will not therefore be of use to international deployments.[5]

Reconnaissance and command and control, though highlighted as priority areas in the Ministry of Defence's reform plans, have not yet received significant boosts. Austria's command-and-control, intelligence, surveillance, target-acquisition and reconnaissance capabilities remain very limited and the country has no combat search-and-rescue capability, strategic-lift capacity or deployable air defence. Austria continues to lack important enablers and the combat-support and combat-service-support capabilities that are needed to conduct more demanding missions.

Very limited resources mean that there is extremely little leeway for further improvements. Between 2004 and 2006, roughly 0.8% of GDP was allocated to defence, or around $300 per capita per year. Among Austria's fellow EU members, only Malta, Luxembourg and Ireland allocate a smaller proportion of GDP to defence. Furthermore, funds are allocated in a way that does not aid efforts to improve Austria's crisis-management profile. In 2006, a full 70% of the defence budget was allocated to meet personnel costs and only 3.8% was spent on investment (procurement and research and development). Investment per soldier actually dropped from €5,379 in 2005 to €2,264 in 2006. The Ministry of Finance does refund some of the direct costs of international crisis management, such as personnel and running costs, but hardly any investment costs.[6] Sustaining deployments while at the same time trying to improve capabilities is difficult, because these goals compete for very scarce resources.

In Germany, international missions have begun to exert an influence on acquisitions and work has been under way to improve capabilities, particularly over the past five years. With the launch of the SAR-*Lupe* satellite in summer 2008, Germany completed its first global satellite-based radar reconnaissance constellation, with all-weather, day and night capabilities. There are plans to purchase five *Global Hawk* unmanned aerial vehicles to replace Germany's manned electronic-reconnaissance aircraft. These are to carry electronic- and communications-intelligence payloads, and it is hoped that they will assume a key role in intelligence, surveillance and reconnaissance. A prototype aircraft is due in 2010, to be followed by four 'production' versions, useable in theatre, to be delivered by 2015. The *Taifun* attack drone will further improve Germany's unmanned aerial capabilities and, together with the *Taurus* missile for the *Tornado* and *Eurofighter* jets, increase its capacity for stand-off precision strikes. Germany now has a deployable headquarters, the Response Forces Operations Command in Ulm, which can run operations up to corps level.

While the German air force is not due to receive its first A400M before 2010, the decision to procure 60 of these military transport aircraft has for the first time secured a strategic-lift capability for the Bundeswehr. All the A400Ms will be equipped with a 'terrain masking' system for low-level flight control and protection against detection by enemy radar, and 24 of them will have additional defence aids. Tanker kits have been ordered for some of the aircraft, with the aim of giving Germany an air-to-air refuelling capability. This is in addition to the planned conversion of the country's existing A310 multirole transport aircraft to enable these too to undertake air-to-air refuelling. Eighty NH90 transport helicopters were ordered in 2000 and 2007 for use by all three Bundeswehr services to enhance in-theatre lift. The *Tiger* support helicopter is to be equipped with precision stand-off anti-tank missiles, and upgrades are planned to extend the in-service life of part of the CH-53 transport-helicopter fleet.

Ground vehicles are also being procured. 201 *Dingo* 2 armoured vehicles will be delivered by 2011 and 272 *Boxer* armoured transport-and-command vehicles have been ordered for delivery beginning in 2008, 72 of which will be ambulance variants. The German army also intends to procure around 400 *Puma* armoured infantry fighting vehicles to equip the 'response and stabilisation' battalions used in crisis management, with delivery beginning in 2009. The forces are also seeking to procure armoured command-and-operations vehicles in four different weight categories. Finally, by 2012, 1,500 ground vehicles are to be upgraded with new command-and-control systems.

In 2004, Germany began procuring units of its new 'system' for equipping soldiers called 'Infanterist der Zukunft' (infantryman of the future), which furnishes individual soldiers with enhanced navigation, communication and protection equipment and weaponry. A further 1,000 units of the system are expected to be procured between 2009 and 2015. In April 2005, the Bundestag approved funding for a new air- and missile-defence system in the form of the Medium Extended Air Defence System (MEADS). MEADS is intended to replace *Patriot* missile systems and to offer better protection from air attacks. Germany has ordered a surface-launched version of the guided IRIS-T missile to use as a secondary missile as part of MEADS. Two counter-rocket, artillery and mortar-round systems have also been ordered to protect troops. The German navy is also expanding its capabilities. Its F122 and F123 frigates are being upgraded and a new frigate class, the F124, entered service in 2006. Four F125s have been ordered for delivery from the end of 2014. New K130 corvettes and U212 submarines, of which five and six have been ordered respectively, have entered service.[7]

This wide range of procurement programmes, though it will not fix all the current shortfalls, would if fully implemented close some important gaps in Germany's capabilities. But German defence expenditure has stagnated in the context of sluggish economic growth, the continuing economic burden of unification and the limits imposed on spending by the euro. From 2004 to 2006, between 1.4% and 1.3% of GDP was allocated to defence – around $38bn annually, or roughly $460 per capita per year. This puts Germany in the lower-middle ranks of EU states as regards the percentage of GDP spent on defence. Regarding the proportions of the defence budget spent on investment relevant to crisis management, Germany is similarly placed among EU states. The Bundeswehr has managed to keep personnel costs stable while gradually increasing its investment rate. In 2006, 57% of the defence budget was allocated to personnel costs and 15.6% was spent on investment. In spite of the overall stagnation of defence spending, investment per soldier rose slightly from €18,250 in 2005 to €19,297 in 2006. Recently, however, plans have emerged to make around $2.69bn worth of cuts to funding for equipment programmes between 2008 and

2011, which would leave an annual gap between procurement plans and available funds of between €1.79bn and €3.26bn. An added difficulty is that current missions are also to be funded out of the defence budget (around €640 million was allocated for international deployments in 2008), although parliament can make alternative arrangements for new missions on a case-by-case basis.

The United Kingdom is the most capable EU member state in terms of its force structure. Capabilities priorities high on the British defence-reform agenda are strategic air and sea lift, carrier strike, precision strike, tactical mobility and force protection. The Ministry of Defence has identified initial-entry and 'shaping' operations (in which future operations are planned out), intelligence, surveillance, reconnaissance, precision-attack, joint land and air offensive operations and post-conflict stabilisation as core priorities to be supported. This translates into a need for improved command-and-control, communications, intelligence, surveillance and reconnaissance capabilities, as well as upgrades or improvements to deployable headquarters, the 'network-enabled' capability, satellite communications, unmanned aerial vehicles, 'future soldier technology' (similar to the 'Infanterist der Zukunft' system described above) and logistics systems. Urgent operational needs that have emerged over the past decade – notably out of operations in Afghanistan and Iraq since 2001 and 2003 – include secure communications (with the US and other allies and between UK forces), intelligence collection and processing, and improved aircraft interoperability.

In a report published in November 2007, the UK's National Audit Office listed no fewer than 20 major procurement projects that had passed 'main gate' (the stage at which the decision about whether to invest in the project is made), and a further ten still at pre-main-gate stage.[8] Between them, the post-main-gate projects cover a wide variety of capabilities. The UK is buying *Typhoon* and *Joint Strike Fighter* aircraft, 25 A400M transport aeroplanes and a number of T45-class air-defence destroyers. Command-and-control, communications, intelligence, surveillance, target-acquisition and reconnaissance capabilities will be bolstered by a variety of acquisitions, including new communications systems (*Falcon* and *Bowman*), *Nimrod* reconnaissance aircraft and the *Watchkeeper* unmanned-aerial-vehicle system, which will provide an all-weather intelligence, surveillance and reconnaissance capability. *Soothsayer* will provide the army with a modern electronic-warfare capability and the UK is also investing further in precision-guided munitions. In addition, main-gate approval was given in 2007 for the acquisition of two aircraft carriers. Projects that

have yet to pass main gate include a future soldier system, further surveillance assets, network-enabled upgrades to the capabilities of frigates and
destroyers to detect, track and engage air targets, the Future Rapid Effect
System of rapidly deployable, network-enabled armoured vehicles, a
strategic tanker aircraft, search-and-rescue and *Future Lynx* helicopters
and a series of logistics and support vessels for the navy (the MARS
programme).

UK defence expenditure has remained relatively stable in recent years,
fluctuating between 2.3% and 2.5% of GDP in the period 2004–06. This
works out to around $50bn–$55bn annually, or an average of roughly $900
per capita per year. This puts the UK in a clear leadership position among
EU states as the state spending the most on defence both as a proportion
of GDP and in absolute terms (2006 figures). The UK is also exceptional
in the way in which resources are allocated within the defence budget.
The country has one of the lowest rates of expenditure on defence personnel and one of the highest investment rates in the EU. In 2006, 40% of the
defence budget was allocated to personnel costs and 24.4% was spent on
investment. Investment per soldier rose from €50,627 in 2005 to €65,027 in
2006, a sum almost 29 times the size of Austria's equivalent investment in
the same year and more than three times that of Germany.

Nonetheless, even with these investment levels it has become clear
that UK defence expenditure is not high enough to support the acquisition
programmes planned. Though efficiency drives are intended to generate
some extra funding, the Treasury's contingency reserve is regularly used
to cover the costs of operational deployments. Contingency funds totalled
£6.6bn between 2001 and 2007, and more than £3.6bn has been spent on
urgent operational requirements since the operations in Afghanistan and
Iraq began. A recent parliamentary report has claimed that operations
costs are beginning to have a negative impact on research and development, suggesting that some long-term funding might need to be redirected
from elsewhere to pay for international operations in order to take pressure off the research-and-development budget.[9]

As far as available means for undertaking and sustaining crisis-
management operations are concerned, the UK is in a different league
to Austria and Germany. This is not to say that the current difficulties
surrounding the funding of acquisitions and the high operational tempo
of British forces do not have an effect. Fundamentally, however, the UK is
in a strong position relative to other EU members, and it seems well-placed
to maintain its high crisis-management profile. In Germany, by contrast,
budgetary shortfalls may limit further improvements, and it is difficult

to see how Austria could significantly improve its performance at current funding levels.

Strategic culture

Different countries' strategic communities have different approaches to the use of armed force, which are largely determined by the country's historical experience.[10] Four defence and security issues in particular stand out as areas on which national strategic cultures diverge. Firstly, states have different views about the relative value of autonomy and cooperation as a basis for security and defence policy. Secondly, states see the primary purpose of the military differently, some favouring territorial defence over force projection and others taking the opposite view. Thirdly, states vary in the emphasis they place on the role of military force in the spectrum of available foreign- and security-policy tools. Finally, countries also differ on their preferred arenas for cooperation, in this context, NATO and the EU.

A country's strategic culture might be an obstacle to high levels of performance in military crisis-management missions if it favoured territorial defence over force projection, civilian over military foreign-policy tools, and autonomy and self-reliance over international cooperation and burden-sharing. In contrast, a strategic culture in which force projection and the use of armed force for foreign-policy purposes were accepted postures and cooperative security and defence frameworks were particularly valued might coincide with high performance levels.

Germany's strategic culture has often been characterised as a 'culture of restraint' (*Kultur der Zurückhaltung*). Whereas most countries refer positively to past military achievements, German strategic culture is founded on a rejection of the country's past and its militaristic excesses. Past German militarism has been invoked on many occasions both within and outside Germany by those wishing to limit the country's assertiveness in the security and defence realm. One particular consequence of the absence of positive reference points for German identity following the Second World War was that national identity soon became closely linked to European integration and NATO, since these frameworks offered the opportunity for integration into the West. German aversion to military force was also reinforced by the powers that occupied the country after the war, and the Cold War fear that Germany could become the battlefield for a nuclear war.

Modern Germany thus has an antimilitaristic and multilateralist outlook. Military force is valued as a deterrent, and its actual use is thus seen as a sign of failure. A framework of civil–military relations based on such principles as the soldier as 'citizen in uniform' and a universal conscription system that has a strong civil, as well as military, component combine with a Bundeswehr whose actions are carefully defined by the constitution (as interpreted by the Supreme Court) to produce a distinctive, civilian-inflected contemporary strategic culture.[11]

Germany has gradually increased its participation in military crisis-management missions since the end of the Cold War. However, more frequent use of the German military does not equal an end to the culture of restraint. Any examination of the intense domestic debate about these military deployments will show that the strategic culture of restraint is still very much alive, even though 'the parameters of "acceptable behaviour" for Germany in the security realm [were] considerably stretched' during the 1990s.[12]

In sum, German strategic culture favours a territorial-defence posture over force projection and the use of civilian over military means to achieve security-policy goals. German multilateralism means that cooperative security institutions are preferred to purely national approaches to security. Regarding the comparative benefits of NATO and the EU, it is unclear whether Germany is more Atlanticist or Europeanist. German political scientist Johannes Bohnen has argued that 'the basic pattern of German defence policy from 1966 onwards has turned on how best to achieve a balance between the US (and Britain) and France'.[13] This implies a German preference for staying more or less equally close to NATO's collective defence on the one hand and the ESDP on the other.

Austrian strategic culture is centred on the idea of neutrality. In 1955, neutrality brought independence to a reunified Austria. Divided into four occupied zones after the war, Austria chose to pledge neutrality in return for regaining sovereignty without having to suffer partition like Germany. Up to that point, Austrian identity and political culture had been characterised by discontinuity. The Second Republic that was established in 1955 came after a long and difficult period in which Austria went from being a great power during the First World War, to an unstable republic incorporated into the German Reich in 1938, to a country occupied by the Allied powers from 1945 to 1955. After this string of discontinuities, neutrality was highly valued as a source of stability.

The discontinuities of the Austrian state had created discontinuities in the role of the country's military, and Austrians grew detached from their armed forces as a result. Furthermore, being on the losing side in both world wars gave Austria an image of itself as weak and of war as unwinnable. It was felt that security could be achieved simply by being neutral.

One consequence of this attitude was a shift towards an 'active' foreign policy, whereby Austria offered its services to other states as a mediator and broker. This approach was seen as the main safeguard of the country's neutrality and, by extension, its security, because it established Austria as a constructive player in the security realm.

Neutrality was incorporated into Austria's constitution on 26 October 1955 by means of a Constitutional Federal Statute:

> For the purpose of the permanent maintenance of her external independence and for the purpose of the inviolability of her territory, Austria of her own free will declares herewith her permanent neutrality which she is resolved to maintain and defend with all the means at her disposal ... In order to secure these purposes Austria will never in the future accede to any military alliances nor permit the establishment of military bases of foreign States on her territory.[14]

The peacetime conduct of a neutral country constitutes a large part of its neutrality policy. The permanent neutral status to which Austria committed itself with the 1955 statute required that in times of peace it not establish ties of any sort that might make neutrality in future conflicts impossible. But in contrast to conduct during war, peacetime conduct is not codified in international law.

When Austria joined the EU in 1995, it was able to subscribe to the full body of EU law, including all the provisions of the Common Foreign and Security Policy, without making any reference to its neutrality. A series of constitutional amendments between 1997 and 2001 gradually eroded the meaning of neutrality. Taken together, these amendments enable Austria to take part in the whole spectrum of Petersberg tasks, including combat missions, even without a UN mandate. They also mean that Austria is not bound by its neutral status as regards the Common Foreign and Security Policy (or the ESDP, which is technically part of the Common Foreign and Security Policy). In 2001, the Austrian parliament stated that 'Austria's status in international law corresponds to that of a non-allied state rather than a neutral state'.[15] From one standpoint, this modified position represents a sensible adaptation to a changing environment in which there are new threats and the role of buffer state between East and West has become redundant.

However, in 2003, a public-opinion survey consulted by a commission on army reform found 69% of the Austrian population in favour of neutrality.[16] Wide public support for neutrality makes it doubtful that

any Austrian government could transform the leverage gained by constitutional amendment into political action. The close association between
neutrality and the post-war Austrian nation as embodied by the Second
Republic, with its prosperity and security, has caused neutrality over time
to become a powerful national myth. Austrian political scientist Karin
Liebhart observed in 2003 that 'In a certain way, neutrality is a symbol for
everything that is connected with the successful foundation and history
of the Second Republic.'[17] As neutrality in Austria has gone from being an
instrument of strategic policy to being almost an end in itself, an heirloom
of Austrian identity, it has become difficult for policymakers to expand
Austrian involvement in international action. The closure of Austrian
airspace to NATO aircraft during the 1999 Kosovo campaign and the 2003
decision to block transit of American troops on their way to Italy from
Germany are reminders that the ongoing fact of Austria's non-allied status
can still impose constraints on military cooperation even though legal
obstacles to it have been cleared away.

In summary, then, Austrian strategic culture creates obstacles to high
performance in crisis-management missions because neutrality has at least
a residual effect on strategic thinking, resulting in a continuing focus on
civilian and diplomatic rather than military means to achieve security-
policy aims and a low estimation of the value of force projection, particularly if it involves combat.

In the UK, in the words of political analyst Andrew Gamble, 'most of
the ... political class, including the bulk of the media, remains attached to a
world role for Britain'.[18] The country's historical experience has bequeathed
to policymakers a sense that the UK's sphere of interests extends beyond
Europe, and that the UK is an important force in the wider world. To an
extent, the sense that 'Britain has been the "gardener" of the international
system, committed to maintaining a perfect lawn and immaculate flower-
beds, always vigilant to weed out unwelcome predators'[19] still underpins
much British strategic thinking. This perception of the UK as a guardian
of global order is partly responsible for the activist character of British
strategic culture, including its broadly positive attitude towards military
intervention. There is in British strategic culture a comparative absence
of taboos against the use of force, and a corresponding pride in having
capable and professional armed forces.[20]

Geography has been central to the formation of these attitudes.
Comparatively secure as an island nation, the UK has traditionally viewed
defence more in terms of the defence of its interests than survival, a matter
of force projection rather than territorial defence. The Second World War

was unusual in this respect as there was a significant threat of German invasion. However, the outcome of that war provided the UK with a major source of positive national myth and memory that bolstered the existing strategic inclination towards activism, including the use of force abroad. Furthermore, the war seemed to many to be proof of the necessity of being prepared to resort to armed force.[21]

Since the end of the war, the United States and NATO have been the UK's preferred partners for international cooperation. In addition to the legacy of its maritime empire, the UK's affinity with the US – embodied in the 'special relationship' – has been a crucial determinant of post-war British defence policy.[22] A close relationship with America served, as Lawrence Freedman has observed, as 'an "influence multiplier" for London' in the post-imperial era.[23] Immediately after the Second World War, British politicians thought of the special relationship as a relationship of equals. While the UK might not have been able to bring as much power to the table as the US, its traditional great-power status and experience were seen as balancing the relationship. British leaders felt that they could offer the materially powerful Americans their political acumen and diplomatic sophistication, won through many decades of great-power status. Thus were the foundations of the transatlantic relationship laid. The related role of transatlantic broker, explaining US policy to continental Europe and vice versa, was also a powerful self-image for the British, and one which reinforced the country's detachment from its European neighbours.[24]

As former UK Ministry of Defence official William Hopkinson has observed, an 'easy assumption' that NATO was central to UK defence and security grew out of the domestic consensus that the UK should maintain close working relations with the US.[25] The sense of a threat from the Soviet Union combined with the idea of the special relationship to produce a strategic outlook that was firmly focused on NATO as the UK's main arena for international cooperation. In a parallel process, British policymakers attempted to frame the UK's comparative remoteness from the process of European integration in terms of the celebrated British preference for pragmatism over grand designs. Appeal to national pride in an imperial past and military successes has also been used by policymaking elites to promote resistance to European integration.[26]

This traditional wariness of the EU notwithstanding, one of the most striking features of British strategic culture is the significant overlap that exists between its own norms and the demands of contemporary military crisis management, including at a European level. The UK's preference for power projection and its enduring perception of itself as a great power with a duty to uphold global order are reflected – albeit in more modest terms – in much of the rationale of modern operations. The UK has a tradition of using its armed forces as a tool of foreign policy alongside civilian tools, and thus has fewer qualms about doing this than other EU member states. Furthermore, British multilateralism has increased over the years of the post-imperial decline in its global influence, with policymakers making extensive use of and promoting cooperative security structures. The 'special relationship' feeds into this, retaining to this day much of its function as an 'influence multiplier' for the UK.

Clearly the traditional tendency for British policymakers to favour NATO over integrated European structures in the security and defence realm sets some limits on the UK's usefulness to the ESDP. Nevertheless, overall, British strategic culture fosters high levels of national performance in international crisis-management missions.

National capacity for action
Domestic public opinion
Public opinion is one of a number of factors that set limits on the options available to national leaders in foreign policy. Of course, mass 'public opinion' as defined and measured by polls and surveys does not precisely reflect the views of a population, and publics are often not well-informed about the intricacies of international crises. Leaders of Western democracies are frequently rather unresponsive to public-opinion data with good reason. Nevertheless, politicians seeking re-election will be careful not to make decisions that run counter to a clearly articulated popular consensus, just as they may use any such consensus to justify decisions.

Providing that the limitations of poll data are kept in mind, it is useful to consult such information for clues about popular threat perceptions, how a society sees the role of its armed forces and what kinds of international mission the public is likely to support. A public that feels secure and has a dim or unspecified perception of international security threats is unlikely to support frequent and demanding international deployments.

Given that public opinion, like the strategic culture of policymaking elites, broadly reflects national preoccupations and norms, we would expect to find the national strategic cultures evoked above broadly reflected in opinion polls. And while data on public opinion is unlikely to have a structuring effect on security policy and performance levels in crisis-management missions, it does serve as an indicator of how much strain the domestic consensus on participation in such missions can take.

Austrians do not as a rule feel threatened, and polling data shows that a large majority of 79% feels 'secure'.[27] When asked in 2008 what they believed were the most important issues for the country, Austrians prioritised inflation (54%), health care (25%) and unemployment (21%). Thus the focus was firmly on domestic issues. Terrorism and defence/foreign affairs were prioritised by very few, polling at 6% and 3% respectively. This poll appeared to show a population with a low threat perception overall. Asked about the most serious problems facing the world, Austrians cited global warming (32%), poverty, food and water scarcity (25%) and international terrorism (14%) as the top three concerns. Armed conflict and nuclear proliferation were mentioned by only 8% and 4% respectively.[28]

The ESDP generally enjoys high levels of public support in EU member states. Austrians are on average more wary, in part because the lingering significance of neutrality to national identity creates concern in the country about the ESDP as a possible source of obligations incompatible with a non-aligned status. When asked in 2000 whether they approved of the European rapid-reaction force planned as part of HG 2003, 63% of Austrians said that they did. Though not a low proportion in absolute terms, this figure represented the third-lowest level of public support for the scheme among the (then) 15 EU members. When asked in 2008 whether defence decisions should be made at a national level or jointly within EU structures, 39% of Austrians favoured national-level policymaking, a larger proportion than the EU average.[29]

A majority of Austrians polled in 2004 supported both Austrian neutrality and the creation of a European army. While this position might at first seem contradictory, it becomes less so when we take into account that most respondents (68%) viewed peacekeeping as being the main function of a European army. Only 20% supported a collective defence obligation on EU states. Public support for international deployments is very much dependent on the type of mission being conducted. While 70% of those polled supported classic peacekeeping missions, which are of long duration but low intensity, only 20% supported peace-enforcement missions, which are higher intensity and of uncertain duration. A full 30% were opposed to international deployments in general, and 50% of those questioned wanted to limit deployments to nearby regions where there were Austrian interests at stake (which would in practice mean the Balkans).[30]

A poll conducted on behalf of the German Ministry of Defence in September and October 2007 suggests that threat perceptions in Germany are, overall, rather low. Some 48% of respondents felt 'secure' or 'very secure' at an individual level. Only 3% felt 'not secure' or 'not at all secure'.

Around 40% of respondents thought that the national security situation was 'secure' or 'very secure'. Furthermore, respondents named as the biggest security risks phenomena that had little to do with traditional security challenges. Some 37% felt 'threatened' or 'very threatened' by 'the global destruction of the environment' and 33% by 'global climate change'. Economic security was a key issue for 30%. War, terrorism and the proliferation of weapons of mass destruction (WMD) all played minor roles in the threat perceptions of these respondents.[31]

When asked in a 2008 European Commission poll what they believed were the most important issues facing the country, only a small minority of German respondents cited international security issues, with 1% citing defence/foreign-affairs issues and 3% citing terrorism. Most, like the Austrians polled in the same survey, were primarily concerned about the domestic issues of inflation (44%), unemployment (35%) and health care (21%). Similarly, when asked what they believed to be the most serious problem facing the world, significantly fewer respondents cited international terrorism (11%), armed conflict (6%) and nuclear proliferation (3%) than cited poverty, food and water scarcity (36%) and global warming (29%).[32]

It should be noted that data for Germany also show that popular threat perceptions are event-driven and hence volatile. For example, public fear that there might be a terrorist attack in Germany increased temporarily in the weeks after the 2001 terrorist attacks on the US and the attacks in Madrid in 2004, only to return to more usual levels shortly afterwards. After the 2005 terrorist attacks in London, however, the threat perception remained elevated, peaking when two suitcase bombs failed to explode on German commuter trains in summer 2006. Whereas in January 2004, only 29% feared a terrorist attack on Germany, by September 2006, the proportion had risen to 61%.[33]

Several polls have pointed to a German preference for tackling problems at a European, rather than a national, level. Seventy per cent of respondents to the 2000 poll mentioned above approved of the idea of a European rapid-reaction force. As in Austria, this is a lower approval rating than the EU average (73%), but in absolute terms the proportion is high. In 2007, Germans viewed terrorism, the environment and defence and security as issues requiring European-level responses (92%, 88% and 81% respectively). The 2008 European Commission poll showed 74% agreeing that defence decisions should be made jointly within the EU.[34] However, it would seem that this openness to multilateral action does not necessarily extend to joint combat operations: a 2007 survey reported that while a majority (63%) of Germans thought it acceptable for the EU to commit more troops to peacekeeping missions, a minority of 16% approved of the EU committing more troops to actions involving combat, echoing Germany's strategic culture of restraint.[35]

Though a very large majority (86%) of Germans polled on behalf of the Ministry of Defence in 2007 took a positive view of the German armed forces, most displayed very little knowledge of the Bundeswehr or the missions in which it was involved. Less than 10% knew even the basic facts about the various international crisis-management missions in which Germany was participating. Support for missions appeared from the survey to be sizeable nonetheless.[36] Such evidence is, however, a useful reminder of the need to treat polling data with some caution. In this case, the survey had rather tendentiously characterised all the missions it asked about either as 'peace' or as 'counter-terrorism' missions. The importance of being sceptical about apparent popular endorsements of interventions is underlined by the fact that another poll taken around the same time as the Defence Ministry survey found a clear majority supporting German with-drawal from Afghanistan. Another poll (by the same pollster) conducted around the same time found only 29% support for ISAF.[37]

There does appear to be a generally negative public response to missions that show unclear results following years of engagement and missions that the public does not feel it understands. Furthermore, some research has suggested that as doubts about the usefulness of particular high-profile missions grow, support for international missions in general tends to drop. One 2007 German poll found 56% of respondents believing that Germany's participation in the war in Afghanistan would increase the risk of terrorist attacks in Germany. While 46% of the poll's respondents had supported international deployments in general in 2005 (with 34% against such deployments), by 2007, this number had fallen to 34%, with a full 50% opposed.[38]

Against this, however, there is evidence to suggest a generally posi-tive disposition among the German public towards a range of international missions: the Ministry of Defence-commissioned poll mentioned above found that a variety of types of mission – ranging from evacuation opera-tions to operations to defend a NATO ally to missions to prevent WMD proliferation – enjoyed significant support. However, here again some scep-ticism is needed: as respondents were asked about hypothetical scenarios, it is possible that positive responses to the idea of intervention came more readily than they might have done in a real-life situation. The methodolog-ical difficulties surrounding the polling data cited here underline the fact that public-opinion polls are never conclusive, and must – despite their undoubted usefulness as broadly indicative tools – not be thought to offer unambiguous guidance.

In the UK, respondents to the European Commission poll conducted in spring 2008 saw crime (38%), immigration (35%) and inflation (19%) as the most important issues facing the country. Terrorism was seen as the main issue by 13%, and defence/foreign affairs was put in top place by a mere 2%. While concern about terrorism is thus more pronounced in the UK than in Austria and Germany, public perceptions of the national agenda are similarly dominated by issues with no (or, in the case of immigration, only indirect) connection to international security challenges. Of the security challenges facing the whole world, global warming (32%) topped the list, followed by international terrorism (23%) and poverty, food and water scarcity (20%). Armed conflict (4%) and nuclear proliferation (2%) were at the bottom of the list of major challenges, as they were in Austria and Germany.

A 2007 'Transatlantic Trends' poll indicated broadly similar threat perceptions. It asked respondents whether they thought they would be personally affected over the next ten years by various security challenges. Grouping together answers to the effect that the respondent believed themselves to be 'somewhat likely' or 'very likely' to be affected by a given challenge gives the following statistical picture: 80% feared global warming; 76% feared the consequences of energy dependence; 68% were concerned about large numbers of refugees and other immigrants entering Europe; 64% were concerned about a major economic downturn; 58% were concerned about Iran acquiring nuclear weapons; 57% feared the global spread of a disease such as avian flu; 50% feared Islamic fundamentalism; and 48% feared international terrorism.[39]

Given British aloofness from the ESDP, it is unsurprising that 55% of Britons polled in the 2008 Eurobarometer survey felt that defence decision-making should take place at a national level, although a full 40% supported joint decision-making at EU level on defence questions. Though public support in 2000 for the creation of an EU rapid-reaction force under HG 2003 was lower in the UK than it was in other EU member states, a majority (60%) still thought the force was a good idea.[40] The 2007 Transatlantic Trends poll showed 76% of British citizens in favour of the EU committing more troops for peacekeeping missions, while the commitment of more EU troops to combat actions did not receive majority support (35%).[41] In indicating broad support for EU peacekeeping but not for combat missions, these results echo German responses, though it is probable that there was different reasoning behind the two sets of answers. Whereas Germans are unlikely to support the deployment of combat troops in general, Britons are more likely to object to their deployment within an EU framework.

A 2006 opinion poll suggested that 81% of Britons felt that the armed forces were overstretched. Interestingly, and in line with the broad British acceptance of the use of armed force for foreign-policy purposes, 54% supported the view that the military should be better resourced and only 36% thought that they should not be asked to do as much.[42] However, regarding the most demanding missions (Afghanistan and Iraq), public confidence that British forces could achieve their goals eroded over time and correspondingly support for these missions dropped markedly. Furthermore, in the case of Iraq, the rationale for going to war in the first place came increasingly under question. A tracking poll comprising data from several polls covering the period 2003 to 2007 shows 53% of the population believing it was right to go to war on the day that combat started, a figure which had risen to 66% by the time coalition forces reached Baghdad in April 2003. However, support plummeted after that point, and the results from 2005 and 2007 show support rates of between 35% and 25%. In 2006, 56% of the population supported British withdrawal from Iraq within 12 months, a proportion that rose to 74% by August 2007. Over the same period support for withdrawal from Afghanistan within 12 months rose from 53% to 65%.[43]

National institutions and decision-making processes
The deployment of troops abroad, although almost always undertaken as part of a multinational operation, is approved at the national level. Each country has its own legal and constitutional framework within which formal approval is given. Some institutional arrangements set more limits than others on the kinds of action national leaders can take. In many European countries, armed forces may be deployed only with prior parliamentary approval, and parliaments may also vote to withdraw troops. In others, participation in international missions is not put to parliamentary vote, and the executive branch of government has the final say. The rights of national parliaments to oversee mission budgets and scrutinise crisis-management plans also vary from country to country. The European Parliament has virtually no power to scrutinise ESDP missions.

The fact that each country has different processes and internal checks on action, and that governments and policies change, introduces an element of uncertainty into the mustering and sustaining of international forces. Decisions can be reversed: for example, Spain and the Netherlands sent troops to Iraq following the 2003 invasion, but subsequent governments pulled them out. In such cases, states' military capabilities are not in question; the uncertainty is about whether the government of the day will opt to make them available.

While most national constitutions stipulate a clear mechanism for the deployment of armed forces abroad, in cases where neither the constitution (if the country has a codified constitution) nor the statute book sets out a decision-making process for deployments, mechanisms are based on customary political practice. In general, constitutional provisions for armed deployment are geared towards declarations of war rather than deployment abroad for other reasons. Hence, several countries have adopted new legislation to adapt to the changed environment.

With a few exceptions in the cases of particular deployment scenarios, prior approval from parliament is needed for deployment abroad in the following EU states: Austria, Bulgaria, Cyprus, the Czech Republic, Denmark, Estonia, Germany, Hungary, Ireland, Latvia, Lithuania, Poland, Romania, Slovakia, Slovenia and Sweden.

In the following 11 countries, a decision from parliament is not required: Belgium, Finland, France, Greece, Italy, Luxembourg, Malta, the Netherlands, Portugal, Spain and the UK. In a few of these states, such as Italy and Spain, it is nevertheless customary for governments to seek parliamentary approval. In France, the constitutional division of powers between the president and the prime minister is unclear, which has in practice resulted in the president having much more power over defence policy, including over decisions to deploy armed forces, than the constitution and relevant laws might suggest.

Substantial parliamentary scrutiny makes it more difficult for governments to sustain high performance levels in international crisis-management missions, simply because the institutional process involves more veto points and thus more necessary compromises. This does not of course mean that high levels of parliamentary scrutiny are undesirable. Indeed, many argue that the restraint they impose is positive.

In Austria, the federal president has ultimate control over the military, but delegates this power to the minister of defence.[44] Article 23 of the constitution affirms the country's commitment to taking an active part in the EU's Common Foreign and Security Policy.[45] Constitutional law states that troops may be deployed abroad to participate in international peacekeeping operations[46] and to fulfil humanitarian and rescue tasks,[47] among other crisis-management operations. The constitution specifies that 'decisions of the European Council on a common defence of the European

Union ... require the adoption of resolutions by the National Council and the Federal Council' (the two parliamentary chambers).[48] Decisions about EU peacekeeping, peacemaking and crisis-management operations require the votes of the federal chancellor and the minister for foreign affairs.[49] If, however, the decision relates to the deployment of Austrian armed forces or civilian personnel, it can only be made via special procedures provided for under constitutional law, which are outlined below.[50]

The law states that the government has the right to deploy armed forces only once it has consulted and been authorised by the Main Committee of the National Council.[51] It does not need the approval of the entire parliament, as it is the Main Committee that is responsible for overseeing the engagement of Austrian troops abroad (with particular responsibility for determining the duration of missions).[52] However, in cases in which the military needs to be dispatched without delay to provide humanitarian aid and rescue support in the aftermath of a disaster or in some other emergency, the federal chancellor and the minister with the portfolio most relevant to the situation may decide to send armed forces without seeking the approval of the Main Committee. In such situations, the Main Committee must be informed immediately and has two weeks in which to challenge the ministers' decision. If the committee mounts a challenge, the deployment must be terminated.[53] (This emergency procedure does not apply to peacekeeping operations.)

Parliament itself may also issue a mandate for an international deployment, which must similarly gain Main Committee approval before going ahead. Parliament also has some say over operational issues, such as the specific budget lines to be used to fund participation in missions, and all members of parliament individually may question the government about missions. Overall, therefore, in Austria, parliament has comparatively strong powers of scrutiny.

In Germany, the minister of defence has control over the armed forces. The operations that the military is authorised to undertake in addition to territorial-defence tasks are stipulated in the country's constitution, called the 'Basic Law'.[54] These include domestic emergencies, in which the armed forces may be used to support the police and to protect civilian property.[55] In the event that German territory or the territory of a NATO ally needs to be defended, the Basic Law gives the Bundestag the authority to declare, following the request of the government and with the consent of the Bundesrat (the parliamentary upper chamber that represents each of the country's states), a 'state of defence'.[56] In a state of defence, control of the armed forces passes to the federal chancellor.[57]

Article 24 of the Basic Law permits the participation of German armed forces in the activities of collective-security systems. It also provides for the possibility of delegating certain state powers to inter-governmental organisations.[58] Decisions about employing the armed forces within systems of collective security and about the deployment of troops in general are approved by the lower chamber of parliament, the Bundestag. Before March 2005, troops could only ever be deployed with prior consent of the Bundestag. In that month, the mechanism was modified by a new law.[59] Now, in certain cases defined as 'urgent' according to legal criteria, armed forces may be dispatched before the consent of the Bundestag has been secured.[60] In such cases, the government must brief the leaders of all the parties in parliament on activities and progress both before and during the deployment.[61] The decision to deploy troops must also be formally submitted to the Bundestag for review as soon as possible. If it declines to give retrospective approval, the troops must be withdrawn immediately.[62] (The law distinguishes between military interventions involving the use of force, and humanitarian missions in which weapons are for self-defence only and soldiers are not expected to engage in combat. Bundestag approval is needed in the first case, but not in the second.[63])

Thus the Bundestag still has the final say in most decisions to use the military abroad. The law is clear that deployment of the armed forces must have the assent of parliament and that this assent may be revoked.[64] Hence, the German armed forces may still be described as a *'Parlamentsheer'*, or 'parliamentary army',[65] though the government now has more flexibility in responding to international emergencies and situations of imminent threat.

For 'low-intensity' international missions, or in situations where the government is seeking an extension of parliamentary approval for a mission, the 2005 law offers a simplified decision-making process. The government's proposal for the mission/mission extension is submitted to selected parliamentary representatives, who may then request a review in parliament. If no such request is made within seven days, parliamentary consent is considered given.[66]

In Germany, parliament has the power to issue a mandate for intervention and must approve deployment in the great majority of cases, but it has limited say over operational decisions, with little input into decisions about which particular budget lines are used to pay for deployments. Like their Austrian counterparts, German members of parliament individually have the right to question the government about a given mission. Overall, there is a high level of parliamentary scrutiny of decisions to participate in international crisis-management missions.

The United Kingdom does not have a codified constitution, relying instead on a body of constitutional law. The constitution thus composed is based on the principle of parliamentary sovereignty. Parliament has the power to change or annul any law by passing an Act of Parliament. The monarch, whose role is essentially ceremonial, appoints a prime minister to head the government, upon proposal by Parliament, and the cabinet exercises executive power on behalf of the monarch.

Due to the absence of a codified constitution, many responsibilities and mechanisms are regulated by unwritten conventions. The fundamental principle concerning the deployment of the armed forces is that the monarch has the power to decide on initiatives brought forward by the government. This royal prerogative (which is in practice exercised by the government itself) is considered the legitimate basis for any military operation: the government does not need to seek parliamentary approval before sending troops abroad. However, government being accountable to Parliament, ministers do inform Parliament, though usually after the fact. This decision-making process has been subject to criticism, especially following British participation in the 2003 invasion of Iraq, when Parliament was given the chance to debate the matter only two days before the war and combat operations involving UK forces began.

In 2006, a report from the House of Lords Select Committee on the Constitution laid out a number of options for increasing Parliament's role in decisions to deploy armed forces. The report considered that 'the exercise of the Royal Prerogative by the government to deploy armed force overseas [was] outdated' and that 'parliament's ability to challenge the executive must be protected and strengthened'.[67] It recommended that, among other things, a joint parliamentary committee should be created to oversee the armed forces, and that some sort of convention should be established for determining the role of Parliament in decision-making about the deployment of the armed forces.[68]

The government responded to the committee's proposals by observing simply that 'The existing legal and constitutional convention is that it must be the government which takes the decision in accordance with its own assessment of the position. That is one of the key responsibilities for which it has been elected.'[69] Thus, for the time being, parliamentary scrutiny of the use of armed force abroad is minimal in the UK. Parliament has no say over mission mandates, the decision to deploy or any operational questions. The right to question the government about missions is held not by individual Members of Parliament but by parliamentary Select Committees. In financial terms, Parliament's powers do not extend beyond control of the general budget.

Linking domestic factors to crisis-management profiles

In the case of the United Kingdom, all the factors outlined are enablers of high levels of ambition and performance. The country's security culture creates an environment favourable towards the use of the military on international missions, public opinion creates a broadly permissive consensus for the use of armed force abroad, and the British political system is characterised by an absence of veto points and comparatively low levels of parliamentary scrutiny, giving governments substantial room for manoeuvre. The wide spectrum of capabilities available to the UK and – despite the difficulties identified above – its relatively healthy funding situation give the country the material resources needed to support high ambition and performance.

In Austria, the situation is very different. Both public opinion and the country's institutional arrangements impose visible constraints on government action. Furthermore, the Austrian armed forces have yet to close significant gaps in capability areas that are crucial for modern operations. Low overall defence expenditure and meagre allocations to investment within the defence budget create a marked tension between the needs of long-term defence reform, including restructuring and re-equipment programmes, and the sustainability of international deployments. In addition, Austria's strategic culture acts as a constraint on high-intensity missions (especially those implemented through NATO), because of the residual power of neutrality as a long-standing tenet of national defence policy. These domestic factors combine to produce the country's comparatively low crisis-management profile. The fact that Austria's crisis-management *ambitions* are not as low as they might be may be due to a growing recognition among the country's policymakers that significant participation in international missions could lend the country greater influence in crisis situations in future. But for the moment, the domestic factors surveyed here illustrate the many constraints acting on policymakers seeking to achieve these ambitions.

The domestic determinants of Germany's international crisis-management profile are also more constraining than enabling. German strategic culture, with its enduring aversion to the use of military force, creates a sensitive political environment in which policymakers are compelled to carefully justify deployments. This is combined with high levels of parliamentary scrutiny further restraining government. Against this, Germany's armed forces do have a wide range of key capabilities (though not at the UK's level) and are moving to strengthen them further, which could point to a raised crisis-management profile in the future. But in the context of plateauing defence budgets, it is unclear whether the financial resources can be found to make the acquisitions envisaged. And though Germany's means could perhaps enable it to do more in the field of crisis management, the antimilitaristic strategic culture, fragile public support for a more active role and the heavily checked-and-balanced political system do not currently support significant steps forward – at the very least, they complicate any agenda for improvement.

CONCLUSION

While demand for international crisis-management forces continues to increase rapidly, the EU is still falling well short of its declared ambitions in this area. Almost ten years of the ESDP have furnished the systems necessary for the Union to be able to assume a more prominent role in global crisis management, including detailed military-technical procedures and a political-strategic framework to guide action. But despite a major expansion in EU forces' geographical and functional reach, in terms of the numbers of troops deployed, ESDP operations have been very limited. The expansion in functional reach has occurred mostly in the realm of civilian crisis management. EU-led (as distinct from NATO- or coalition-led) operations have only covered a small portion of the possible ESDP task spectrum. And while these operations have been successful within the very limited parameters set for them, they have also evidenced the lack of determination among member states to attain commonly agreed goals. This problem is most clearly seen in the difficulties experienced with force generation.

It is often said that the EU lacks capabilities and political will. It is important to remember, however, that the EU is not a state in its own right, and that both its capabilities and the will to use them ultimately come from its constituent states. Most of the reasons for the disconnect between the EU's ambition and reality can be found in the capitals of member states, not in Brussels. Together, member states' ambitions for and performance in crisis management – their crisis-management profiles – determine the EU's capacity for action. These are, in turn, shaped by domestic factors, several of which exert strong countervailing pressures on governments to those exerted by the international security environment and the demands of the ESDP. As a result, overall, commitment to making the ESDP a success is weak.

As the groundwork for a high-functioning ESDP has already been laid by Brussels – ironically, perhaps, under the direction of the very same capitals that are failing to sufficiently commit to the policy – the onus is firmly on member states to move things along. Analysis of crisis-management profiles reveals an enormous range of ambitions and performance across European states. Among those countries whose ambitions and performance are aligned, output varies dramatically. In other states, ambitions outrun performance. This is a particular cause for concern, as it means that false expectations are generated. The problem of false expectations is currently replicated at the level of the EU itself.

Clearly, ambitions and performance are not just determined by what a country has the material means to do. The argument of this paper has been that the scope for action afforded by a country's decision-making systems and institutions, its national strategic culture and its broader domestic norms about involvements abroad are, together with the available material means, the primary domestic determinants of a state's commitment to international missions. If these national pressures largely complement those of the international environment, levels of ambition and performance will be high; if they conflict with them, they will be low. Detailed scrutiny of the domestic characteristics of the three sample states of the United Kingdom, Germany and Austria has shown that domestic factors can play an enabling role for crisis management, as in the case of the UK; a mostly constraining one, as in Germany's case; or, as in the Austrian case, an almost completely constraining one.

The limits imposed by national factors on international action have profound implications for the EU's capacity to contribute to international crisis management. It is unrealistic to expect national crisis-management profiles to converge upwards in the near term. Even assuming states' political leaders wanted to make determined efforts to modify their national strategic cultures and decision-making institutions, and bolster their key capabilities, change could only be effected gradually over time. National constraints can be expected to present significant obstacles to the implementation of the ESDP for some time yet. The UK's preference for operating in international frameworks other than the ESDP shows that such constraints can come from countries with high levels of ambition and performance as well as from lesser performers.

The EU's best hope of raising its game in the near to medium term may therefore lie in enabling some sort of leadership group to act within the ESDP framework. This kind of idea was mooted in the 'permanent structured cooperation' within the ESDP that was envisaged in the Lisbon Treaty.[1] Such an arrangement would allow a group of EU member states to define more ambitious targets – for example, in the field of capabilities development – and pursue them in cooperation with each other within the EU framework without creating an obligation on member states that either did not want to sign up to the group or were not in a position to do so. In return for participation in the group, governments could expect enhanced political weight in crisis-management decision-making.

Small-group leadership is a sensitive issue in the EU: intergovernmental policymaking in the Union has traditionally set a high value on inclusiveness, sometimes to the detriment of effectiveness. But whether or not the Lisbon Treaty enters into force, the creation of some kind of crisis-management avant-garde within the Union is probably needed in order to encourage states to contribute more. The balance between inclusiveness and effectiveness would of course still need to be struck because, in the end, they are two sides of the same coin – legitimacy. Thus, any group would need to operate on the principle that the criteria for joining, which would be based on states' crisis-management ambitions and performance, should be less demanding than the criteria for staying in the group. The goal would be to encourage member states individually to do more, not for all of them to perform at more or less the same level as before. In this way, the sum of EU effort could turn out to be greater than its original parts.

NOTES

Introduction

1   See Richard Gowan, 'The Strategic Context: Peacekeeping in Crisis, 2006–08', *International Peacekeeping*, vol. 15, no. 4, 2008, p. 457; Center on International Cooperation, *Annual Review of Global Peace Operations 2008* (Boulder, CO: Lynne Rienner, March 2008); Adam Roberts and Dominik Zaum, *Selective Security: War and the United Nations Security Council since 1945*, Adelphi Paper 395 (Abingdon: Routledge for the IISS, 2008), p. 54.

2   Council of the European Union, 'A Secure Europe in a Better World: European Security Strategy', December 2003, p. 15.

3   Roberts and Zaum, *Selective Security: War and the United Nations Security Council since 1945*, p. 30.

4   Michael E. O'Hanlon, *Expanding Global Military Capacity for Humanitarian Intervention* (Washington DC: Brookings Institution Press, 2003), p. 48.

5   Reinhard Trischak, 'Status Quo/ Perspectives in Civilian, Police and Civil–Military Capabilities Development within the EU and Cooperation with CHG 2008', presentation, Berlin, 23 April 2007, p. 2.

6   See Council of the European Union, 'A Secure Europe in a Better World: European Security Strategy'.

7   Nick Witney, 'Re-Energising Europe's Security and Defence Policy', European Council on Foreign Relations policy paper, July 2008, p. 9.

8   James Dobbins et al., *Europe's Role in Nation-Building: From the Balkans to the Congo* (Santa Monica, CA: RAND, 2008), p. 234.

9   See Helmut Fritsch, 'EUFOR RD Congo: A Misunderstood Operation?', Queen's Centre for International Relations, Martello Paper no. 33, 2008; Witney, 'Re-Energising Europe's Security and Defence Policy'.

10 Council of the European Union, 'EU Concept for Force Generation', Doc. 10690/08, 16 June 2008, p. 5.

11 Witney, 'Re-Energising Europe's Security and Defence Policy', p. 43.

12 Fritsch, 'EUFOR RD Congo: A Misunderstood Operation?', p. 34, see also p. 46.

13 Heinrich Brauss, 'The Future of Defence Planning – A NATO Perspective', in Sven Biscop and Franco Algieri (eds), *The Lisbon Treaty and ESDP: Transformation and Integration*, Egmont Paper 24 (Brussels: Academia Press for Egmont – The Royal Institute for International Relations, June 2008), p. 38.

14 Heiko Borchert, Johann Frank and Gustav E. Gustenau, 'Politischer Wert/ Nutzen von Engagements im Bereich des internationalen Krisenmanagements

unter besonderer Beachtung von Beiträgen und Entwicklungsoptionen des österreichischen Bundesheeres', Austrian Ministry of Defence, 'Beiträge zur Sicherheitspolitik' [security policy papers], January 2006.

15 Borchert, Frank and Gustenau, 'Politischer Wert/Nutzen von Engagements im Bereich des internationalen Krisenmanagements unter besonderer Beachtung von Beiträgen und Entwicklungsoptionen des österreichischen Bundesheeres', pp. 10–13.

16 Julian Lindley-French, 'The Revolution in Security Affairs: Hard and Soft Security Dynamics in the 21st Century', *European Security*, vol. 13, nos 1–2, 2004, p. 12.

17 The 2003 European Security Strategy cites international terrorism, the proliferation of WMD, failing states, organised crime and regional conflicts as the key current security threats. See Council of the European Union, 'A Secure Europe in a Better World: European Security Strategy', pp. 3–5.

18 The same is the case with equivalent policies undertaken by NATO.

19 On the conduct of negotiations at these two levels, see Andrew Moravcsik, 'Integrating International and Domestic Theories of International Bargaining', in Peter B. Evans, Harold K. Jacobsen and Robert D. Putnam (eds), *Double-Edged Diplomacy: International Bargaining and Domestic Politics* (Berkeley, CA: University of California Press, 1993); and Putnam, 'Diplomacy and Domestic Politics: The Logic of Two-Level Games', in *ibid.*

20 See European Defence Agency, 'An Initial Long-Term Vision for European Defence Capability and Capacity Needs', October 2006, pp. 10–11.

Chapter One

1 Council of the European Union, 'A Secure Europe in a Better World: European Security Strategy', p. 11.

2 *Ibid.*, p. 14.

3 *Ibid.*, p. 11.

4 Council of the European Union, 'Presidency Conclusions', Cologne European Council, 3–4 June 1999, p. 66, http://ue.eu.int/ueDocs/cms_Data/docs/pressData/en/ec/57886.pdf.

5 'Presidency conclusions' are summaries of the proceedings of EU Council meetings, published by the holder of the EU presidency.

6 Council of the European Union, 'Presidency Conclusions', Helsinki European Council, 10–11 December 1999, http://ue.eu.int/ueDocs/cms_Data/docs/pressdata/en/ec/ACFA4C.htm.

7 Council of the European Union, 'Process for the Elaboration of the Headline and Capability Goals', Doc. 6756/00, 14 March 2000.

8 External Relations Council, Council of the European Union, 'Declaration on EU Military Capabilities', 9379/03 (presse 138), 19–20 May 2003.

9 Council of the European Union, 'Headline Goal 2010', endorsed on 17 and 18 June 2004, p. 1, http://ue.eu.int/uedocs/cmsUpload/2010%20Headline%20Goal.pdf.

10 Bernard Kouchner, opening speech to EU–NATO seminar, Paris, 7 July 2008.

11 Council of the European Union, 'A Secure Europe in a Better World: European Security Strategy', p. 7.

12 Council of the European Union, 'Civilian Headline Goal 2008', Doc. 15863/04, 7 December 2004, p. 3.

13 Council of the European Union, 'Civilian Headline Goal 2008: Questionnaire on Contributions from Non-EU States towards the EU Civilian Crisis Management Capability under ESDP', Doc. 12208/06, 14 August 2006; Center on

International Cooperation, *Annual Review of Global Peace Operations 2008*, p. 9.

14 See Council of the European Union, 'Final Report on the Civilian Headline Goal 2008', Doc. 14807/07, 9 November 2007; Council of the European Union, 'New Civilian Headline Goal 2010', Doc. 14823/07, 9 November 2007.

15 The Military Committee is made up of chiefs of defence and other military representatives of member states. The function of the committee is to provide direction to the EUMS and military advice to the Political and Security Committee, which also has a major role in crisis-management mission planning, and to make recommendations to the latter, either on its own initiative or at the committee's request. The EUMS – whose personnel is mostly seconded from the member states – performs three main functions: early warning, situation assessment and strategic planning for the crisis-management tasks laid out in the TEU. Though the EUMS works under the direction of the Military Committee, it is organised as a department of the Council Secretariat.

16 For a rundown of these scenarios and an outline of the military planning process, see also 'EU Military Capability Development', presentation by Colonel L.F. Lunigiani, EUMS, http://www.baks.bundeswehr.de/portal/PA_1_0_P3/PortalFiles/02DB040000000001/W274QLLS742INFODE/eums130607+esdp+orientation+course.pdf?yw_repository=youatweb.

17 Interviews, Brussels, April and July 2008.

18 Council of the European Union, 'EU Concept for Logistic Support for EU-led Military Operations', Doc. 10963/08, 19 June 2008, pp. 10–11.

19 Substitution missions involve EU personnel assuming some executive roles in the crisis-afflicted region by taking on tasks, such as policing, that are usually undertaken by the state. In the stabilisation and reconstruction scenario that does not include a substitution mission, the role of EU personnel would be limited to mentoring and advising roles.

20 The CHG 2008 final report itself highlights this fact. See Council of the European Union, 'Final Report on the Civilian Headline Goal 2008', p. 19.

21 See note 15 for more information on these bodies.

22 See Dobbins et al., *Europe's Role in Nation-Building: From the Balkans to the Congo*, p. 215.

23 See *ibid.*, p. 235.

24 See Council of the European Union, 'Force Strength by Nations in AOO: 3247', http://www.consilium.europa.eu/uedocs/cmsUpload/Force_Stenght_by_Nations_in_AOO.pdf.

25 Interview, Brussels, July 2008.

26 Kees Homan, 'Operation Artemis in the Democratic Republic of Congo', in European Commission, 'Faster and More United? The Debate about Europe's Crisis Response Capacity', 31 May 2007.

27 United Nations Security Council, 'Deuxième rapport spécial du Secrétaire général sur la Mission de l'Organisation des Nations Unies en République démocratique du Congo', S/2003/566, 27 May 2003.

28 The following paragraphs are based on Ståle Ulriksen, Catriona Gourlay and Catriona Mace, '*Operation Artemis*: The Shape of Things to Come?', *International Peacekeeping*, vol. 11, no. 3, Autumn 2004.

29 The following account of EUFOR RD Congo is based on a report from the EU Operations Headquarters Potsdam, 'Operation EUFOR RD Congo', February 2007.

30 See also conclusions in Homan, 'Operation Artemis in the Democratic Republic of Congo'; Ulriksen, Gourlay and Mace, '*Operation Artemis*: The Shape of Things to Come?'; and Fritsch, 'EUFOR RD Congo: A Misunderstood Operation?'.

31 Witney, 'Re-Energising Europe's Security and Defence Policy', p. 41.

Chapter Two

1   IISS, *The Military Balance 1995/96* (Oxford: Oxford University Press for the IISS, 1995).

2   IISS, *The Military Balance 2008* (Abingdon: Routledge for the IISS, 2008).

3   IISS, *The Military Balance 1995/96*.

4   IISS, *The Military Balance 2008*.

5   Ministry of Defence of France, *Défense et Sécurité nationale: Le Livre Blanc* (Paris: Odile Jacob/La documentation française, June 2008).

6   Ministry of Defence of the United Kingdom, 'Strategic Defence Review: Modern Forces for the Modern World', July 1998.

7   Ministry of Defence of the Czech Republic, 'Military Strategy of the Czech Republic', 2005.

8   Jaak Jõerüüt, Minister of Defence, Estonia, 'National Military Strategy: Annex to the Government of the Republic Regulation No. 10 from 18 January 2005 on Implementation of the National Military Strategy (unofficial translation)', para. 51, accessible from http://www.mod.gov.ee/?op=body&id=369; Estonian Ministry of Defence, 'Estonian Participation in International Operations', 30 May 2006, http://www.mod.gov.ee/?op=body&id=249.

9   Ministry of Defence of France, '2003–2008 Military Programme Bill of Law', 2002, pp. 7–8, http://merln.ndu.edu/whitepapers/France_English.pdf.

10   Ministry of Defence of France, *Défense et Sécurité nationale: Le Livre Blanc*, p. 211.

11   The UN Standby Arrangements System is a system whereby UN member states put specified resources on standby for rapid deployment for use in UN peacekeeping operations. Pledged resources are requested as needed by the UN Secretary-General and approved by the participating member states.

12   Ministry of Defence of Germany, 'Weißbuch zur Sicherheitspolitik Deutschlands und zur Zukunft der Bundeswehr', 2006, pp. 84–6.

13   Ministry of Defence of Romania, 'Strategia de Transformare a Armatei Romaniei', 2007, pp. 14–15, http://www.mapn.ro/documente_cheie/strategie_transformare_2007.doc; Romanian Chief of Army Staff Lieutenant-General Ioan Sorin in 'Mapping the Future: World Army Chiefs Look to the Future', supplement to *Jane's Defence Weekly*, 4 October 2006, p. 12.

14   Ministry of Defence of Slovenia, 'Slovenian Defence Reform', unpublished document provided to the IISS, 2007.

15   Ministry of Defence of the United Kingdom, 'Delivering Security in a Changing World: Future Capabilities', CM 6269, July 2004, pp. 14–18.

16   *Ibid.*

17   Major-General Wolfgang Wosolsobe, Austrian Military Representative to the EU, presentation to expert seminar 'The Lisbon Treaty and ESDP: Transformation and Integration', Egmont Palace, Brussels, 28–29 April 2008; Johann Frank, *Perspektiven der europäischen militärischen Integration: Entwicklungsszenarien und Konsequenzen für Österreich* (Vienna: Internationales Institut für Liberale Politik, 2007), p. 39.

18   Ministry of National Defence of Lithuania, 'White Paper: Lithuanian Defence Policy', 2006, pp. 19, 31–4.

19   Ministry of Defence of the Netherlands, 'Service Worldwide', 2007, pp. 14–15.

20   IISS, *The Military Balance 2003/04* (Oxford: Oxford University Press for the IISS, 2003); IISS, *The Military Balance 2004/05* (Oxford: Oxford University Press for the IISS, 2004); IISS, *The Military Balance 2005/06* (Abingdon: Routledge for the IISS, 2005); IISS, *The Military Balance 2006* (Abingdon: Routledge for the IISS, 2006); IISS, *The Military Balance 2007* (Abingdon: Routledge for the IISS, 2007); *The Military Balance 2008*.

21   Ministry of Defence of Bulgaria, 'Military Strategy of the Republic of Bulgaria', 2002, http://www.mod.bg/en/koncepcii/

military_strategy.html; Ministry of Defence of Bulgaria, 'White Paper on Defence', 2002, http://merln.ndu.edu/whitepapers/BulgariaEnglish.pdf; Ministry of Defence of Bulgaria, 'Armed Forces Modernization Plan 2002–2015', 2002, http://www.mod.bg/en/modern/plan.html; Ministry of Defence of the Czech Republic, 'Military Strategy of the Czech Republic', 2005; Ministry of Defence of Denmark, 'Defence Agreement 2005–2009', 2004; Ministry of Defence of Denmark, 'Memorandum: Consolidated Implementation Basis for "Danish Defence Agreement 2005–2009"', 7 December 2004; Jõerüüt, Minister of Defence, Estonia, 'National Military Strategy: Annex to the Government of the Republic Regulation No. 10 from 18 January 2005 on Implementation of the National Military Strategy (unofficial translation)'; Ministry of Defence of Estonia, 'Estonian Participation in International Operations', 30 May 2006, http://www.mod.gov.ee/?op=body&id=249; Ministry of Defence of France, 'Projet de loi de programmation militaire 2003–2008', 2002; Ministry of Defence of Germany, 'White Paper 2006 on German Security Policy and the Future of the Bundeswehr', 2006; Ministry of Defence of Greece, 'European Security and Defence', 2007; 'Interview: Lt-Gen. Zolatan Szenes, Chief of the Defence Staff, Republic of Hungary', *Jane's Defence Review*, 13 October 2004, p. 34; 'Ferenc Juhász: Hungary's Minister of Defence', *Jane's Defence Weekly*, 24 August 2005; István Biró, 'The National Security Strategy and Transformation of the Hungarian Defence Forces', research paper, US Army War College, 18 March 2005; Ministry of Defence of Italy, 'Chod's Strategic Concept', 2004, http://merln.ndu.edu/whitepapers/Italy_Eng-2004.doc; Ministry of Defence of Latvia, 'National Armed Forces Medium-Term Development Plan for the Period 2005–2008', 2005; Ministry of Defence of Latvia, 'Report to the Parliament on National Defence Policy and National Armed Forces Development in 2006', 2006; Ministry of Defence of Latvia, 'Latvian Security and Defence Policy in 2006', *Baltic Security and Defence Review*, vol. 9, 2007; Ministry of National Defence of Lithuania, 'White Paper: Lithuanian Defence Policy', 2006; Ministry of National Defence of Lithuania, 'Guidelines of the Minister of National Defence 2007–2012', 2007, http://search.delfi.lt/cache.php?id=64838696E6F133DD; Ministry of Defence of the Netherlands, 'Service Worldwide', 2007; correspondence with the Polish Institute of International Affairs, February 2008; Polish Chief of Defence Staff Franciszek Gagor, statement to hearing of the National Defence Commission of the Sejm, 10 January 2008, *Bulletin of the National Defence Commission*, no. 5, http://orka.sejm.gov.pl/Biuletyn.nsf/0/0EA43B6BFD2ED02AC12573DB003A783C/$file/0015106.pdf (in Polish); Ministry of Defence of Romania, 'Strategia de Transformare a Armatei Romaniei', 2006; Ministry of Defence of Romania, 'The Endowment Conception with Major Equipment and Systems of the Romanian Military 2006–2025', 2006; Ministry of Defence of Slovakia, 'Security Strategy of the Slovak Republic', 2005; Ministry of Defence of Slovakia, 'Slovak Armed Forces', 2007, pp. 4–5; Ministry of Defence of Slovenia, 'Slovenian Defence Reform'; Ministry of Defence of Spain, 'Strategic Defence Review', 2003; Ministry of Defence of the United Kingdom, 'Delivering Security in a Changing World: Future Capabilities'; Major-General Wolfgang Wosolsobe, Austrian Military Representative to the EU, presentation to expert seminar 'The Lisbon Treaty and ESDP: Transformation and Integration'; Frank, *Perspektiven der europäischen militärischen Integration: Entwicklungsszenarien und Konsequenzen für Österreich*; Government of Finland, 'Finnish Security and Defence Policy 2004', Government Report 6/2004, 2004; Department of Defence of Ireland, 'White

Paper on Defence', February 2000, http://
www.defence.ie/website.nsf/72804bb47
60386f380256c610055a16b/93191a155924
dad5802570c8005065d3/$FILE/whiteppr.
pdf; Department of Defence of Ireland,
'The White Paper on Defence: Review of
Implementation', February 2007, http://
www.defence.ie/website.nsf/fba727373c
93a4f080256c53004d976e/e1cd6e42fd36e
bbf802572b4003b7368/$FILE/WPReview.
pdf; Government of Sweden, 'Our Future
Defence – The Focus of Swedish Defence
Policy 2005–2007', Swedish Government
Bill 2004/05:5, http://www.sweden.gov.
se/content/1/c6/03/21/19/224a4b3c.pdf.

22   IISS, *The Military Balance 2008*.
23   Calculated from data in IISS, *The Military Balance*, various editions.
24   *Ibid.*
25   IISS, *The Military Balance*, various editions.
26   See Dieter Schadenböck, 'Separation of Parties by Force (SOPF)', *Truppendienst* [Austrian armed forces journal], no. 300, issue 6 of 2007.
27   See Slovenian Press Agency (STA), 'Slovene Daily Notes Kosovo Mission's New Responsibilities', 14 February 2007.

28   'NATO's Role in Afghanistan', rush transcript by Federal News Service of interview with James L. Jones at Council on Foreign Relations, 4 October 2006.
29   'NATO's Afghan Mission: Stressed and Strained', IISS *Strategic Comments*, vol. 12, issue 8, October 2006.
30   'Die Deutschen müssen töten lernen', Spiegel Online, 20 November 2006; 'NATO's Role in Afghanistan'.
31   See House of Commons Defence Committee, 'UK Operations in Afghanistan: Thirteenth Report of Session 2006–07', HC 408, 18 July 2007, p. 18 and Ev. 85.
32   House of Commons Defence Committee, 'The Future of NATO and European Defence: Ninth Report of Session 2007–08', HC 111, 20 March 2008, p. 37.
33   House of Commons Defence Committee, 'UK Operations in Afghanistan: Thirteenth Report of Session 2006–07', Ev. 56.
34   House of Commons Defence Committee, 'UK Operations in Afghanistan: Thirteenth Report of Session 2006–07', Ev. 10.
35   Quoted in 'Die Deutschen müssen töten lernen'.

Chapter Three

1   Data on defence expenditure in this section is drawn from IISS, *The Military Balance 2008*.
2   For more details see IISS, *European Military Capabilities: Building Armed Forces for Modern Operations* (London: IISS, 2008) and IISS, *The Military Balance 2008*.
3   European Defence Agency, 'National Defence Expenditure in 2006', November 2007, http://www.eda.europa.eu/genericitem. aspx?area=Facts&id=309.
4   Borchert, Frank and Gustenau, 'Politischer Wert/Nutzen von Engagements im Bereich des internationalen Krisenmanagements

unter besonderer Beachtung von Beiträgen und Entwicklungsoptionen des österreichischen Bundesheeres', pp. 16–17.
5   Martin Agüera, 'High Hopes for Defense Reform: Austrians Seek More Money for Procurement', *Defense News*, 21 February 2005; Joris Janssen, 'Austria Receives First *Dingo* 2', *Jane's Defence Weekly*, 18 May 2005; Georg Mader, 'Austria Receives *Typhoon* But Concerns Persist over Cuts to Programme', *Jane's Defence Weekly*, 18 July 2007.
6   In the case of UN crisis-management missions, the situation tends to be less difficult, as the UN itself refunds fixed

sums per person and unit of equipment to contributing nations every six months.

7   Andrew White, 'Germany Orders KMW Grizzly Prototype', *Jane's Defence Weekly*, 27 June 2007; Damian Kemp, 'Germany Plans *Global Hawk* Purchase', *Jane's Defence Industry*, 7 February 2007; White, 'Germany to Upgrade 1,500 Vehicles with FuInfoSys Heer', *Jane's Defence Weekly*, 10 January 2007; Christopher F. Foss, 'Germany Orders *Skyshield* for C-RAM Role', *Jane's Defence Weekly*, 11 April 2007; Foss, 'Germany Moves on GFF Group 1 Vehicles', *Jane's Defence Weekly*, 1 February 2006; Foss, 'Germany Moves on GFF Group 2 Vehicles', *Jane's Defence Weekly*, 18 January 2006; Foss, 'Germany Unveils its *Puma* IFV Demonstrator', *Jane's Defence Weekly*, 10 May 2006; Nicholas Fiorenza, 'Germany – Wide Aspirations', *Jane's Defence Weekly*, 8 November 2006; Alex Pape, 'Germany Signs for F125 Frigate Production', *Jane's Navy International*, 1 September 2007; Richard Scott, 'Germany Buys Callisto Submarine Communications System', *Jane's Navy International*, 1 July 2007; Michael Nitz, 'Germany's *Magdeburg* Begins Sea Trials', *Jane's Navy International*, 1 June 2007; Joris Janssen Lok, 'Dutch Deliver P3Cs to Germany', *Jane's*, 2006; Pape, 'Germany Completes Frigate Procurement Project', *Jane's Navy International*, 1 June 2006; Robin Hughes, 'Germany Opts for Surface-Launched IRIS-T to Complement MEADS', *Jane's Missiles and Rockets*, 1 July 2007; 'Germany Orders PARS 3 LR Anti-tank Missiles', *Jane's Missiles and Rockets*, 1 August 2006; Keri Smith, 'Germany Chooses Rheinmetall for NBS Development', *Jane's Defence Industry*, 1 May 2007; Pape, 'Germany Opts for Eurocopter Deutschland to Upgrade CH-53G Helicopters', *Jane's Defence Industry*, 1 April 2007.

8   For the full lists see UK National Audit Office, 'Ministry of Defence: Major Projects Report 2007', 30 November 2007.

9   IISS, *The Military Balance 2008*, p. 108.

10 For more on strategic culture in Europe, see Bastian Giegerich, *European Security and Strategic Culture* (Baden-Baden: Nomos, 2006); Christoph Meyer, *The Quest for a European Strategic Culture: Changing Norms on Security and Defence in the European Union* (Basingstoke: Palgrave Macmillan, 2006).

11 John S. Duffield, 'Political Culture and State Behavior: Why Germany Confounds Neorealism', *International Organization*, vol. 53, no. 4, August 1999; Adrian Hyde-Price and Charlie Jeffery, 'Germany in the European Union: Constructing Normality', *Journal of Common Market Studies*, vol. 39, no. 4, November 2001; Arthur Hoffmann and Kerry Longhurst, 'German Strategic Culture and the Changing Role of the Bundeswehr', *WeltTrends*, no. 22, Spring 1999; Longhurst, *Germany and the Use of Force: The Evolution of German Security Policy 1990–2003* (Manchester: Manchester University Press, 2004); Hans J. Reeb, *Sicherheitspolitische Kultur in Deutschland seit 1990*, WIFIS Aktuell no. 31 (Bremen: Edition Temmen, 2003).

12 Hoffmann and Longhurst, 'German Strategic Culture and the Changing Role of the Bundeswehr', p. 162.

13 Johannes Bohnen, 'Germany', in Jolyon Howorth and Anand Menon (eds), *The European Union and National Defence Policy* (London: Routledge, 1997), p. 51.

14 'Federal Constitutional Law of 26 October 1955 on the Neutrality of Austria', http://www.ris.bka.gv.at/erv/erv_1955_211.pdf.

15 'Resolution by the Austrian Parliament: Security and Defence Doctrine', 12 December 2001; see also Gustenau, 'Towards a Common European Policy on Security and Defence: An Austrian View of Challenges for the "Post-Neutrals"', European Union Institute for Security Studies, Occasional Paper 9, October 1999.

16 See Bundesheerreformkommission, 'Bundesheer 2010: Bericht der Bundesheerreformkommission', 2004, p. 105.

17 Karin Liebhart, 'Austrian Neutrality: Historical Development and Semantic

Change', in András Kovács and Ruth Wodak (eds), *NATO, Neutrality and National Identity: The Case of Austria and Hungary* (Vienna: Böhlau Verlag, 2003) p. 33.

[18] Andrew Gamble, *Between Europe and America: The Future of British Politics* (Basingstoke: Palgrave Macmillan, 2002), p. 232.

[19] International Centre for Security Analysis, 'Coalitions and the Future of UK Security Policy', Royal United Services Institute, Whitehall Paper no. 50, 2000, p. 8.

[20] Stine Heiselberg, 'Pacifism or Activism: Towards a Common Strategic Culture within the European Security and Defence Policy?', Danish Institute of International Affairs, Working Paper 4/2003, 2003, p. 28.

[21] Hyde-Price, 'European Security, Strategic Culture, and the Use of Force', *European Security*, vol. 13, no. 4, 2004; Brian C. Rathbun, *Partisan Interventions: European Party Politics and Peace Enforcement in the Balkans* (Ithaca, NY: Cornell University Press, 2004), p. 81.

[22] Lawrence Freedman, *The Politics of British Defence, 1979–98* (Basingstoke: Palgrave Macmillan, 1999).

[23] *Ibid.*, p. 55.

[24] Michael Howard, 'Afterword: The "Special Relationship"', in William Roger Louis and Hedley Bull (eds), *The Special Relationship: Anglo-American Relations since 1945* (Oxford: Clarendon Press, 1986); William Wallace, 'The Collapse of British Foreign Policy', *International Affairs*, vol. 81, no. 1, January 2005.

[25] William Hopkinson, *The Making of British Defence Policy* (London: Stationery Office, 2000), pp. 38–9.

[26] Oliver J. Daddow, *Britain and Europe since 1945: Historiographical Perspectives on Integration* (Manchester: Manchester University Press, 2004), p. 2.

[27] Susanne Giesecke and Friederike Strebl, 'Country Report on Austria', FORESEC consortium, 19 June 2008.

[28] European Commission, 'Eurobarometer 69: Public Opinion in the European Union', June 2008.

[29] Franz Kernic, Jean Callaghan and Philippe Manigart, *Public Opinion on European Security and Defense: A Survey of European Trends and Public Attitudes Toward CFSP and ESDP* (Frankfurt am Main: Peter Lang Verlag, January 2002), p. 50; European Commission, 'Eurobarometer 69: Public Opinion in the European Union'.

[30] See Borchert, Frank and Gustenau, 'Politischer Wert/Nutzen von Engagements im Bereich des internationalen Krisenmanagements unter besonderer Beachtung von Beiträgen und Entwicklungsoptionen des österreichischen Bundesheeres', p. 22.

[31] Rüdiger Fiebig and Thomas Bulmahn, 'Sicherheits- und verteidigungspolitisches Meinungsklima in der Bundesrepublik Deutschland', Sozialwissenschaftliches Institut der Bundeswehr, 19 November 2007, http://www.bundeswehr.de/portal/ PA_1_0_P3/PortalFiles/C1256EF40036B05B/ W2794BZP715INFODE/Umfrage+SOWI+ 2007.pdf?yw_repository =youatweb.

[32] European Commission, 'Eurobarometer 69: Public Opinion in the European Union'.

[33] Institut für Demoskopie Allensbach, 'Terroranschläge in Deutschland? Die Mehrheit ist Besorgt', Allensbacher Berichte, no. 14, October 2006.

[34] European Commission, 'Eurobarometer 68: Public Opinion in the European Union', Autumn 2007, pp. 2, 33; European Commission, 'Eurobarometer 69: Public Opinion in the European Union', p. 95.

[35] German Marshall Fund of the United States and Compagnia di San Paolo, 'Transatlantic Trends: Key Findings 2007', http://www. transatlantictrends.org/trends/doc/ Transatlantic%20Trends_all_0920.pdf

[36] See Fiebig and Bulmahn, 'Sicherheits- und verteidigungspolitisches Meinungsklima in der Bundesrepublik Deutschland'.

[37] Renate Köcher, 'Der Preis der Freiheit und der Sicherheit', *Frankfurter Allgemeine Zeitung*, 16 October 2007.

[38] *Ibid.*

[39] German Marshall Fund of the United States and Compagnia di San Paolo, 'Transatlantic Trends: Key Findings 2007'.

[40] European Commission, 'Eurobarometer 69: Public Opinion in the European Union';

Kernic, Callaghan and Manigart, *Public Opinion on European Security and Defense: A Survey of European Trends and Public Attitudes Toward CFSP and ESDP*, p. 50.

41 German Marshall Fund of the United States and Compagnia di San Paolo, 'Transatlantic Trends: Key Findings 2007'.

42 YouGov, 'YouGov, *Daily Telegraph* Survey Results', fieldwork 24–26 October 2006, http://www.yougov.com/uk/archives/pdf/TEL060101020_3.pdf.

43 See YouGov, 'Iraq Trends', 15 June 2007, http://www.yougov.com/uk/archives/pdf/trackerIraqTrends_060403.pdf; YouGov, 'YouGov, *Daily Telegraph* Survey Results', fieldwork 24–26 October 2006; YouGov, 'YouGov, *Sunday Times* Survey Results', fieldwork 9–10 August 2007, http://www.yougov.com/uk/archives/pdf/results%2007%2008%2010%20Iraq.xls.pdf.

44 See 'Federal Constitutional Law', Article 80, http://www.ris.bka.gv.at/erv/erv_1930_1.pdf.

45 *Ibid.*, Article 23f.

46 'Bundesverfassungsgesetzes über Kooperation und Solidarität bei der Entsendung von Einheiten und Einzelpersonen in das Ausland', KSE-BVG, BGBl, I, Nr 38/1997, 1997, http://ris.bka.gv.at/taweb-cgi/taweb?x=d&o=l&v=bgbl&db=BGBL&q=%7B$QUERY%7D&sl=100&t=doc4.tmpl&s=(I%2038/1997):PORG, § 1, 1, (a).

47 *Ibid.*, § 1, 1, (b).

48 'Federal Constitutional Law', Art. 23f (1).

49 *Ibid.*, Art. 23f (3).

50 *Ibid.*, Art. 23f (4). The details of these procedures are laid out in 'Bundesverfassungsgesetzes über Kooperation und Solidarität bei der Entsendung von Einheiten und Einzelpersonen in das Ausland'.

51 'Bundesverfassungsgesetzes über Kooperation und Solidarität bei der Entsendung von Einheiten und Einzelpersonen in das Ausland', § 2, 1.

52 *Ibid.*, § 2, 6.

53 *Ibid.*, § 2, 5.

54 'Grundgesetz für die Bundesrepublik Deutschland', Article 87a, 2, http://www.bundestag.de/parlament/funktion/gesetze/grundgesetz/gg.html.

55 *Ibid.*, Article 87a.

56 *Ibid.*, Article 115a.

57 *Ibid.*, Article 115b.

58 *Ibid.*, Article 24.

59 'Gesetz über die parlamentarische Beteiligung bei der Entscheidung über den Einsatz bewaffneter Streitkräfte im Ausland' ('Parlamentsbeteiligungsgesetz'), BGBl, I, S. 775, 18 March 2005, http://bundesrecht.juris.de/parlbg/BJNR077500005.html.

60 'Parlamentsbeteiligungsgesetz', § 5, 1.

61 *Ibid.*, §§ 5, 2, 6, 1.

62 *Ibid.*, § 5, 3.

63 *Ibid.*, § 2, II.

64 *Ibid.*, §§ 1, II, 3 and § 8.

65 The German Constitutional Court coined this term in its rulings on overseas deployments of the armed forces.

66 'Parlamentsbeteiligungsgesetz' §§ 4, I, 7.

67 House of Lords Select Committee on the Constitution, 'Waging War: Parliament's Role and Responsibility', 15th Report of Session 2005–06, Volume I: Report, HL Paper 236–I, 27 July 2006, p. 41.

68 *Ibid*, p. 42.

69 'Government Response to the House of Lords Constitution Committee's Report "Waging War: Parliament's Role and Responsibility"', CM 6923, 7 November 2006.

Conclusion

1 Sven Biscop, 'Permanent Structured Cooperation and the Future of ESDP: Transformation and Integration', forthcoming in *European Foreign Affairs Review*, vol. 13, no. 4, 2008.

⌐IISS ADELPHI PAPERS

RECENT **ADELPHI PAPERS** INCLUDE:

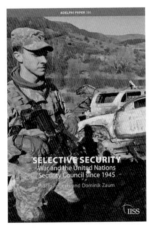

ADELPHI PAPER 395

Selective Security: War and the United Nations Security Council since 1945

Adam Roberts and Dominik Zaum

ISBN 978-0-415-47472-6

ADELPHI PAPER 396

Abolishing Nuclear Weapons

George Perkovich and James M. Acton

ISBN 978-0-415-46583-0

All Adelphi Papers are £15.99 / $28.95

For credit card orders call **+44 (0) 1264 343 071** or e-mail **book.orders@tandf.co.uk**

Routledge
Taylor & Francis Group